# BICYCLE CAMPING

by Diana Armstrong
photographs by John Kelly

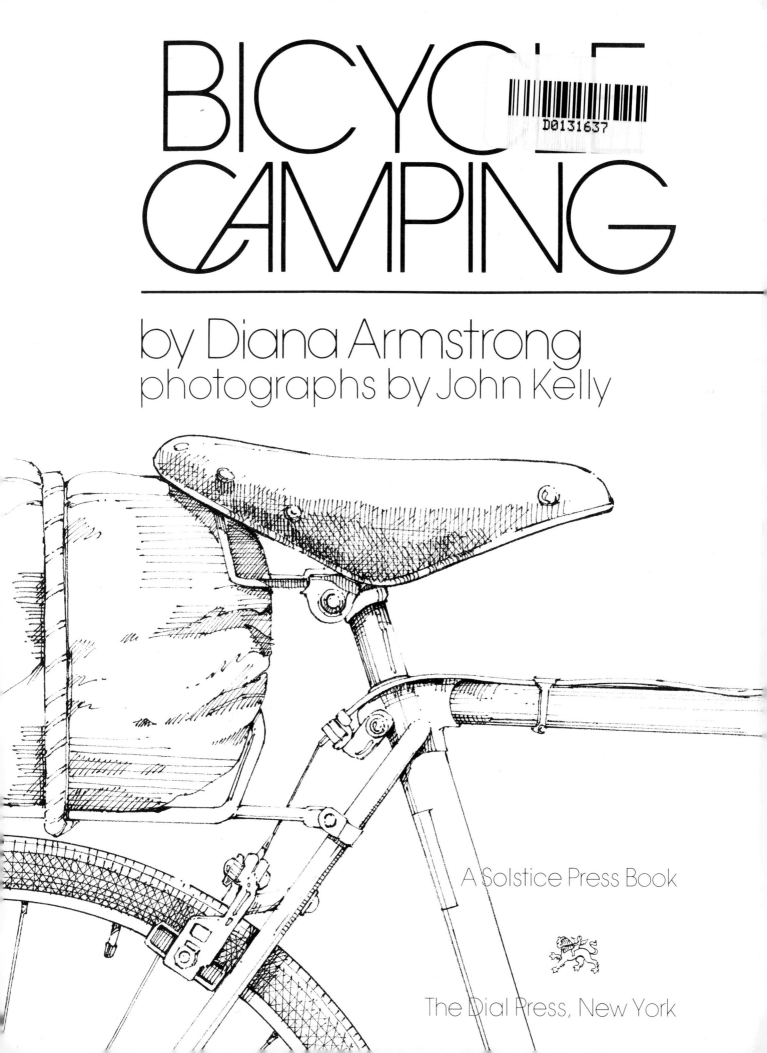

A Solstice Press Book

The Dial Press, New York

Dedicated to all my teachers, especially
those curled on both sides of me now,
my parents and my children.

Published by
The Dial Press
1 Dag Hammarskjold Plaza
New York, New York 10017

© 1981 by North Country Book Express, Inc.

All photographs in this book, except
where credited, were taken by John Kelly.

A Solstice Press book produced at North
Country Book Express, Moscow, Idaho, by
Ivar Nelson and Patricia Hart.

Designed by Dana Sloan.

Manufactured in the United States of America
First Printing
Library of Congress Cataloging in Publication Data

Armstrong, Diana.

    Bicycle camping.
    "A Solstice Press book."
    1. Bicycle touring. I. Title.
GV1044.A75    796.6    80-20893

ISBN 0-8037-0790-8

# Preface

# Thanks

Transportation by bike is embraced as a good idea but generally rejected as a serious one in North America where people persist in believing that transportation begins and ends with the family car. Suburbia, the child of this arrangement, grows bigger and bigger but never grows up.

We have a lot of bikes, between 82 and 89 million are in use (or not in use). About 10 or 11 million will be sold this year. To be ridden? Or left to rust as a troublesome toy. Driving our cars, we fall into believing that we are independent of our environment—an arrogant assumption. We must change. Increased bike use and more energy-efficient cars may be our best bets for relieving our energy and pollution problems. Automobile drivers should bear the real costs of their activities.

It's doubtful that many people decide to go bike touring in order to save gas. The reasons are more personal: fun, adventure, relaxation, togetherness, solitude, to lose weight, lose the blues. But whatever the reason, the result is that use of the "most benevolent of machines" (S.S. Wilson) makes little demand on material and energy resources, contributes little to pollution and greatly to health. We are designed not to be moved, but to move ourselves. And to enjoy ourselves as organism, as body/spirit, to move rather slowly.

Diana Armstrong
August 1980
Moscow, Idaho

Appreciation is extended to the following for their help: Tina Foriyes (English Department, University of Idaho, Moscow, Idaho), F. James Futterer (Velo Sport Cyclery, Cheney, Washington), Roger Ames (Velo Sport, Moscow, Idaho), Tim Young (Two Tyred Tour, Jackson, Wyoming), and the folks at J.P.'s Bike Shop and Northwest Mountain Sports in Moscow, Idaho.

# Contents

# PREPARATION

Of all the cyclists I have met, the one I remember most vividly is Lucky Nolan. He's serious about his cycling, to the tune of about eighty pounds of gear methodically attached to a heavyweight ten-speed that had known finer days as a five-speed. In the front basket (not rack, not alloy) is a metal thermos (the kind steelworkers swing to lunch), a canteen, a huge flashlight and several wrapped and tied packages of Lord knows what. Attached to the upright handlebars is a large headlight and rearview mirror. To the top tube is fastened a length of 4-inch plastic sewer pipe which carries ten pounds of tools. In the giant rear baskets is a large canvas tent, cotton sleeping bag, Coleman stove, gallon of fuel, several more flashlights, the headlight battery, an axe, five pounds of coffee, canned soup, a fishing creel, and finally the fishing pole itself, rising triumphantly from the mess like a tulip in springtime. Dressed in denims, cowboy boots, and workshirt, topped with a hat emblazoned with fishing flies, and surrounded by an aura of roll-yer-own, Lucky bikes and fishes, fishes and bikes.

"Army forced me to retire," he confided, "wouldn't let me work or drive. But I fooled 'em. Bought a bike. I ride 2000 miles every summer here in Colorado."

It might appear that the biking has gotten lost under the fishing, maybe under outwitting the Army, maybe under all the crazy gear. But the bike is there. It's the base; it's transportation. Recreation, escape, indulgence and mystique it may also be, but first of all, it's transportation.

He walks a lot, too—down as often as up. He sleeps in the afternoon, fishes in the morning and evening, and rides at night. I felt light as a newborn nymph when we parted, me on my double-butted tubing, neatly festooned with little more than thirty pounds of mostly feathers and nylon, pedaling in next-to-lowest gear while Lucky walked his joy up Poncha Pass. The next day we met again. I caught up with him about noon. He had fished, taken a promising detour, and slept a few hours. Magic. Plucky Lucky Nolan. God bless.

While I would never recommend his approach to equipment, I surely do like Lucky's attitude. Getting ready for a bike camping trip can be overwhelming. The amount and variety of information about bicycling is surprising. The array of equipment available is astounding. Combining bicycling and camping seems like asking two scruffy giants to share a trundle bed. Preparation is a process of selective learning. While planning my first tour, I wanted to be open to the un-expected, like a soldier of fortune, yet well-prepared, like the good scout on the calendar in our childish hearts.

You don't have to know everything about bikes and the world before you make your first bike camping trip. You don't have to be rich, young, or even skinny. Just enthusiastic.

1

# When

Usually, life does not revolve around plans for a bike trip. Time must be wrested from the daily rut. It is when you get off or get out, when someone can take the kids, when you have the money, when you are not in school, or when you can't stand it another minute. Usually, that's summer, when motorists are tourists, too.

If you are working full-time, you can always quit. For my first tour, I did, and spent the first few weeks of my salvaged summer resting and getting into "shape," that elusive, mythical state. Then I toured for four weeks. Subsequent trips have not had such dramatic preludes. I've simply left when I could and returned when I had to. Once you've undertaken one tour, it's easier to take another, and before you know it, bike touring will become an activity integrated with the rest of your life.

# Where

Making a loop from your home to someplace and back, using the bicycle as transportation from beginning to end, is very appealing. However, a trip which combines the bike and motorized transportation is more common.

You can build a tour around having to be some particular place by a certain date. For example, some friends of mine had planned to drive to Ashland, Oregon, to attend several plays at the Shakespeare Festival. They could provide me a ride home. Ashland, then, became my destination. Perhaps a general area of the country or a particular national, provincial, or state park interests you, or you would like to visit special people in your life. Be aware of weather and traffic conditions, such as heat in the desert or crowds in the major parks.

Wherever you decide to cycle, you may want to follow a route that has been recommended by a cyclist or even designed with cyclists in mind. Cycle touring organizations can suggest such routes. The information may be as sparse as a photocopied road map with annotations. Detailed guidebooks and large-scale maps are available for well-known cycling routes and trails. Well-traveled routes are usually selected for their combined features of scenery, historical interest, and safety. For more information, see the References section in the back of this book.

# How Long

Once a tentative route has been selected, you may want to know, more or less, how long it will take to complete. Most 10-year-olds can ride 50 miles a day in flat terrain. Eighty miles may not be too much for a grown-up. If conditions are tough, 30 miles will be a challenge. A day with downhills, tailwinds, and cool sunshine can push you over a century before you know it. You should plan for a day each week of zero miles to provide for rest and replenishment, enjoyment of special places, and time for fixing equipment.

If a 50-mile daily average won't get you to where you have to be by a certain date, go ahead and plan for 75-mile days. If you are a "practicing cyclist," strong, spirited, and the owner of a good bike, you can probably do that many miles. The trip will be more enjoyable, however, if extra days are found for it, rather than turning it into a time trial.

Don't worry about your body wearing out. During the first three to five days, it may complain a lot and act incensed at the new demands, but soon it will settle down. Bike camping is a lot of fun. You may never want to stop. The satisfaction of arriving at your destination is very fulfilling but is quickly diluted by knowing that there are no more miles to ride, that this simple and healthy way of spending your vacation is over.

Financial resources, unlike thigh size and cardiopulmonary function, do not usually build up while you tour. Commitments made before you left are still there when you return. They determine how long you can tour.

# Style

Consider your purpose. Is it better met by traveling alone or with others? Or just one other? Is it better met by carrying a lot of cash and little camping equipment or the other way around? I like to tour alone because my normal life is rich, and occasionally riddled, with family and friends. Being alone is a luxury and a rarity. I am more relaxed moving at my own erratic pace and on my own peculiar time. I don't have to consider anyone but myself.

The lone cyclist is more vulnerable to attack, but is also more readily protected by strangers. Although you might appear strange to them, four-wheeled vacationers, storekeepers, and residents feel comfortable approaching you because you are alone. They seem more eager to offer information and ask questions.

Advertisements in local bike shops and various cycling periodicals should turn up fellow travelers. For short trips, touring companions are usually abundant, but if you can't find a companion, don't be afraid to go alone. Solo touring is often more a

matter of intention rather than reality, anyway. On summer tours in the United States and Canada, you often meet other cyclists. Your paths will merge for a day or two, then separate.

Traveling with a friend or a group can be a social experience in the best sense of the word. Many of the cyclists I have ridden with have been more experienced than I was at the time. I observed and learned, trying to match my pedaling speed to theirs, noting when they shifted, what they wore and ate, and how they maneuvered in traffic. Tools can be shared and the weight of special or common equipment divided between riders in the group. Then, an extra sweater, rain protection, or book of stories can be brought along. Common chores can be divided, too. Cooking and setting up the tent can happen simultaneously, as can going to the laundry, fixing a flat, and shopping for groceries. Frisbees, flutes, harmonicas, songs, poems, ghost stories, games, and massage are tucked away in abundance in the packs, fingers, and minds of your companions. The disadvantage of group touring is that many opinions must be considered before making decisions and the possibility of "problems" is greatly increased.

A tour sponsored by an organization in the business of providing tours can solve a lot of the problems encountered on group rides. Leadership and mechanical expertise is part of the package. A list of organizations that sponsor domestic and foreign bike tours is published yearly by Bikecentennial and *Bicycling* magazine (see the References section of this book).

# Cost

Cost is part of planning the when, where, and how of your trip. It is possible to go touring with just a sweater and a credit card. It is also possible to be nearly self-sufficient, with stove, tent, and a rugged individualistic outlook. Although I tend toward the self-contained style, I like to eat in cafes, less for the flavor of the food than of the locale. If you plan to buy most of your food in grocery stores but eat in cafes once a day, count on spending at least $10 a day.

Minimum cost of lodging is zero, but don't go counting on it. I look for a free place first, but if the free place isn't available, then I must pay. Campgrounds often have qualities that I am more than willing to pay for. Bring enough money for an occasional motel room, too. Also bring enough for replacing worn-out or broken bike parts, for laundry, showers, swimming pools, hot springs, cold beer, and plenty of food.

Another expense is the cost of getting yourself and your equipment to the place of departure or home from the point of termination. This may involve a separation of you and your bike. Bus, train, or plane all entail taking the bike apart to some degree, packing it in a box, and reassembling it at the other end. There is the risk that your machine may be damaged by handling in transit.

Procedures for shipping bikes change and may vary from one place to another, even within the same transportation system or company. Call ahead and determine the policy of the airline, train, or bus you will be using. Perhaps the best approach is to write the main office for company policy and come armed with a copy of it. Just hand it to the clerk. Some airlines will not accept bikes at all because of the number of damage claims they have had to pay. Most charge between $15 and $20 for shipping and supply a strong crate. The bike is charged as excess baggage.

Amtrak charges $4 (1980) for handling. Greyhound will accept a boxed bike as regular baggage with the price of your ticket, but if it is lost or damaged, you cannot make a claim. For that protection, the bike must be sent as freight.

I have moved several bikes long distances by paying someone who was driving that way to carry it. The drivers are happy to have a silent, gas-paying passenger, and I don't have to pack the bike. Of course, there is no way to guarantee reimbursement for damage or loss, and you have to trust the driver.

Moving a bike on a car-mounted rack is convenient and more than one bike can be carried, but the bikes will be exposed to the elements. I prefer to keep my bike in the car and make provisions for carrying luggage outside. The least desirable rack is the bumper-mounted style because the bikes are subjected to exhaust and matter churned up from the road. Protect the bikes by wrapping them in plastic or making room for them in the car, particularly in road construction areas. A roof-mounted rack will keep the bikes cleaner, but don't forget they are on top when you drive into the garage. A roof rack, which is quite expensive, can be made for much less, but don't scrimp. It may be carrying thousands of dollars worth of bicycles.

# Children

   If you can direct their energy all in one direction, children do very well touring. But a child is still a child, whether at home or on the road, and has special needs as a cyclist. Adults can get by with less food and rest than optimum, but a child needs lots of both. Adults may prefer the spontaneity of an unstructured trip, but a child needs the security of structure. An easily frustrated child at home will be no less so touring. He or she even may be more subject to discouragement. Patience is needed by the adult tourers, and everyone should agree to a slower pace. Let the child lead, too. Also helpful is adoption of a child-like attitude. Remember how tired you got as a kid doing *anything* all day long? Stop frequently in order to keep up enthusiasm for the routine of daily riding.

   When my youngest son was nine, we rode a hundred miles in two days, a first for both of us. His bike was a small-wheeled and heavy ten-speed. His training consisted of riding his bike a couple of miles to school each day. At the end of the first day, totaling 45 miles, he was exhausted and mad at me for my crazy ideas. Totally fatless, he lacked the supply of fuel his mom had in abundance. But after a hot bath, eight hours of sleep, and three meals, he was ready to go again. I chose a different route home that was longer, but safer. I maintained that the distance was "about the same." He was happy and spirited on the quiet road that spun through the wheat fields.

   A child's energy is like a bouncing ball—incredibly variable. A child must be kept filled with food, encouragement, and sometimes, hot air.

# Women

Cycling and swimming are the two sports that women's performances most closely approach those of men. When aerobic capacity is measured in terms of liters of oxygen consumed per minute per kilogram of muscle, there is no difference between men and women. A gram of female muscle is just as effective as a gram of male muscle, given equal training. But since most women have less muscle than men, the best women athletes usually have less aerobic capacity than the best men athletes. Women age more slowly than men however, and may therefore lose their aerobic capacity more slowly. A small but strong cyclist can excel climbing hills. Women have a lower center of gravity than men and their muscle mass is concentrated in the legs. The female knee joint is more stable. These factors may contribute to equalizing performance and endurance between the sexes.

I am often asked, "Were you bothered?" meaning was I sexually assaulted, when people hear of my lone cycling adventures. The answer is no. No, I've never been hurt. I'm cautious, lean, and mean. But I have been saluted by a couple of exhibitionists. And once out of fear, I changed my campsite. It was a good thing, too, because later that night the two men who had aggressively questioned and looked me over earlier, returned. I watched from my position of safety, far up the hill in the trees, as they failed to find me. Pay attention to your intuition.

Another time, I had a blowout near Rock Springs, Wyoming, a town of no average reputation. If I could pick my places to have a blowout, Rock Springs would not be it. But I was glad to have the opportunity to try out my new special foldable spare tire. I wrestled and struggled uselessly to get it over the rim. Feeling stupid and female, I waved down a truck driver (easy to do near Rock Springs). He wrestled and struggled to get it over the rim. He failed and CB'd a buddy behind him, who stopped and together they conquered the recalcitrant clincher. The moral of this story is to make sure all your stuff works before you leave home. Make sure you can take care of yourself but know that people are usually exceedingly friendly and helpful.

It is your right to tour alone, male or female. Be careful and expect harassment. Don't be afraid to stop traffic, call the cops, scream, or prosecute.

*Stalfarfar—the Swedish grandfather who became a legend traveling from Lapland to Rome.*

# The Older Cyclist

Rune Hassner

Bicycling is an ideal form of exercise for an older person. As we get older, we should cycle more, not less, and eat less, not more. Pedaling can be easier than walking, but exercise is the goal.

An older person is often retired and has time during the day. Shopping and errands don't have to be tacked on to the end of a frantic workday. Riding a bike can fill time, rather than kill time.

All cyclists, and especially older people, should avoid congested areas. Responses become slower as we age. The quick maneuvers that riding in traffic requires become more difficult. An older person, when injured, heals more slowly.

Exercise slows the aging process, but over-doing it is as dangerous as not getting any exercise at all. A yearly physical examination and doctor's advice about undertaking an exercise program is a good idea for the person past middle age. Professional opinion should be sought, especially if regular, vigorous exercise has not been a part of one's life.

For the beginning older cyclist, upright handlebars are probably more desirable than the dropped bars. Buy a bike that fits the physical shape and satisfies the purpose, not one that matches all the pretty pictures in the ads. The older rider may feel more secure on tires that are at least 1 1/4-inches wide. A three-speed with its internal gears may be preferred because shifting is so easy. Are you going on long tours? Do you have to ride up and down steep hills? If not, you don't need a ten-speed.

On the other hand, older cyclists may feel that they deserve a lot of gears to go

# Fitness

with their hard-earned gray hairs. A twelve- or fifteen-speed with a high gear of 95 and a low of 25 can provide unrestricted cycling pleasure. A bicycle built for two (well-built with a wide range of gears) is the perfect entertainment for an older couple.

On long trips, an older cycle tourist may want to vary his or her exercise by walking up steep hills. Pushing a loaded bike uphill isn't a piece of cake. If it is easier and more efficient to walk, there is no reason not to.

Staying in motels and hostels may be more to an older tourist's taste than camping out. Cycling guarantees exercise whether or not the bike is loaded and the cyclist sleeps out of doors.

The goal of training before cycle touring is to be "fit enough" to enjoy the tour. You won't if you are in pain, day after day, that gets worse instead of better. You won't enjoy touring if your actual performance falls far short of your expected performance.

Cardiopulmonary or cardiorespiratory fitness refers to the capacity and efficiency of heart, lungs, and blood vessels. Regular exercise, such as cycling, makes the system more efficient. Lung and heart capacities increase and each beat of the heart delivers more oxygen. The capillary network increases and the heart doesn't have to beat so often at rest or during exercise. Blood pressure stays down and muscles become better able to use oxygen from the blood. The muscles in the legs, which are the body's largest blood-pumping accessory, become larger and make the heart's work easier.

The American College of Sports Medicine recommends training at least three days a week, continuously for 15 to 60 minutes, using 60 to 90 percent of maximum heart rate or 50 to 80 percent of maximum oxygen uptake, to develop and maintain cardiorespiratory fitness. Maximum heart rate can be determined by subtracting your age from 220. In other words, ride hard and ride often.

# Training

While a training program depends upon any individual's current condition and goals, a general conditioning program for a long tour might consist of the following routine:

Beginning about four to six weeks before leaving, ride five miles a day for six days, then rest one day. During the next week, ride ten miles in one hour each day for six days, and rest the seventh. In the third week of training, ride 25 miles for three days, alternated with ten-mile days, and one day of rest. The week before leaving, ride fifty miles at least twice, in five or six hours on an unloaded bike. Load the bike and ride fifty miles in eight hours. Select a varied terrain for training, and hope that wind, rain, cold, and heat will occasionally accompany you.

Activities such as running, hiking, swimming, skating, rowing, cross-country skiing, jumping rope and various ball games improve cardiopulmonary fitness. These activities employ continuous and rhythmic movement and are considered

Bill Woolston

aerobic. Keep in mind, however, that cycling is the best overall exercise in preparation for a bike trip.

Deep-knee bends should be avoided because full flexion of the knee is damaging. Strengthening the muscles around the knee will help to prevent soreness and strain. The following exercise strengthens the quadricep: sit on a table with your feet resting on a chair about eight to ten inches lower than the table. With a weight (begin with five pounds) fastened to your ankle, straighten the knee and hold for ten seconds. Rest for ten seconds. Do three sets of ten repetitions. The hamstring can be strengthened by fastening a weight to one ankle, standing on the other leg, and lifting the weighted ankle by flexing the knee to a right angle. Hold for ten seconds and rest for ten. Do two sets of ten repetitions. As strength increases, increase the weight.

Sit-ups (bent-knee style) strenghthen the lower back. Tai Chi and yoga develop balance, flexibility, and sensitivity. They also greatly aid circulation and bring peace of mind. Learn a routine of stretches that feels good to you.

A training program can be incorporated into your daily life more easily than you might think. Commuting to work, riding to school, and running errands, particularly riding an old one- or three-speed, can supply a lot of exercise. Before a tour, I take all the long and hard ways to my various destinations in town. Sometimes this involves gravel roads and steep hills that I have to stand up and pedal to get over. Another of my particular training exercises is a time trial. Using either my three-speed or my ten-speed, I start at a corner where the bank clock gives me the time. I ride to a corner in the next town where another bank gives me the time. I have no idea if the clocks are synchronized. The time is "my time," and I work to reduce it.

Mental preparation is also very important. Highly individual, it may include "announcing" your plans to friends and associates. The public aspect may serve to strengthen your resolve. Talking to people who have cross-country cycled is very encouraging. Don't be discouraged by motorists who are appalled at your vow to make a flimsy machine with no motor or roof go a thousand miles. Make sure you are well rested before you begin your trip. Many cyclists have recurring bad dreams of physical injury before starting the tour. They will disappear once on the road. Expect difficulty, yes, but deal with it as part of the experience—just another hill to climb.

Brooks McKinney, one of the tandem team members who rode across the country from Santa Monica to New York in ten days, twenty-one hours and forty-five minutes counsels: "Despite all rational plans for optimizing the chances of success, ultimate control of the mission lies with the forces of fate, nature, and time. All you can do is prepare to accept, and deal with, whatever comes up."

# Diet

Your body's requirements for cycling or for working in the daily grind are not qualitatively different. Several tests have studied the effect of diet on endurance and used bicycling to measure the results. In 1968, a Swedish scientist tested nine athletes after three-day periods on three different diets: high protein and fat; high carbohydrate; and a mixture of carbohydrates and protein. Each subject was tested after the experiment to insure that the differences could be accounted for only by diet. The average endurance of the subjects on the high protein diet was three times less than that of those on the diet approximating a typical vegetarian diet. The mixed-diet subjects were halfway in between.

A diet composed mainly of whole grains and whole grain products, vegetables, legumes, fruits, and fish is ideal. A high-protein diet does not increase muscle energy or build strong muscles. Exercise does not increase the need for protein. Only work builds muscle. The daily requirement of protein is small, partly because fuel for energy comes largely from carbohydrates and fats and partly because protein liberated from damaged cells is resynthesized into new

protein. An excellent source of protein is tofu, a product made from soy beans. It contains little fat and is readily digestible, though it is not readily available in all grocery stores.

Carbohydrates should make up most of the dietary intake, particularly when exercising vigorously, such as on a cycling tour. Lots of pasta, bread, and cookies is more than a sedentary person needs, but a cycle tourist will burn the calories up. It is recommended that the carbohydrate intake be increased to 60 to 65 percent of the diet a few days before the beginning of a tour to elevate the amount of glycogen stored in the muscle cells. Carbohydrate stores (glycogen) are used for strenuous activity and are depleted fairly quickly.

Stored fat is available as fuel in greater abundance than carbohydrates. Through training, the body's burning of fat can be made more efficient. It is estimated that a cyclist with limited training will burn approximately 45 percent fats, 45 percent carbohydrates, and 10 percent protein on long, easy rides. Through conditioning, the body will learn to burn about 60 percent fats, 30 percent carbohydrates, and 10 percent protein.

The way to train the body to use its fat stores is to go on long, steady, six- to eight-hour rides. While riding, don't replenish the carbohydrate supply. Cut food intake to one-third of normal, but continue to drink lots of water. In training for a long tour, deplete your carbohydrate stores on a couple of 50-mile rides. Fasting is an excellent way to teach the body to use its stored resources. When fasting, continue to exercise, but not strenuously. Take nice, long walks or cycle only short distances. Avoid drinking undiluted juices with a high sugar content. Drink broth and herb teas as well as juices. Stressing your body this way can be very valuable. It is possible a situation could arise on tour in which you would have to ride your bike without food for a length of time longer than desirable for comfort and safety. If you have learned to burn fats efficiently, your body will adjust to the stress more easily.

If you want to lose weight by cycling, you will have to ride hard and still curtail your appetite when you get home. Remember Rousseau's advice that temperance and labor are our two best physicians. One alone is not as effective as the two combined. If you eat 2200 calories a day, and cycle an hour a day at 20 mph for six days a week, you will lose two pounds a week. Eat 2700 calories, and you will lose only one pound. If you must have that double dip ice cream cone, you can cycle an hour before or after your indulgence and you will come out even.

While everyone is concerned about his or her diet, what one eats is a very personal matter. In order to achieve high performance in cycling or other activities, it is necessary to follow a diet which avoids certain foods and emphasizes others. Decide what is best for you.

# Packing

Weighing down a bike with 25 to 70 pounds of gear should be done with thought, practice, and reflection. A trained road racer could probably ride 12 mph on a BMX with flat tires towing a wagon full of army surplus camping equipment. Most tourists, however, are pleasure seekers and are, therefore, concerned with weight and resistance.

People generally take more than they need. My advice is to start out with the minimum amount of baggage to make the first few days as easy a ride as possible. You can always add a sweater, book, or pound of gorp later.

Thirty pounds should be enough for summer touring where food is readily available. Forty to fifty pounds would include a stove, raw ingredients, shoes, larger tent, and extra clothes for cold weather and rain. Sixty to seventy pounds is probably necessary for transcontinental trips across several latitudes, through various climates, and through isolated stretches. For global touring, every one of the seventy pounds racked and lashed onto the bike may be required, but it is a general principle of touring that you do not have to carry everything you need. The webs of civilization run everywhere and run deep. You are connected to groceries, to phones, and, eventually, to a bike shop.

Bicycles are designed to carry 45 percent of the weight on the front wheel and 55 percent on the rear. Therefore, when packing, attempt to maintain that distribution. Divide the weight in the same ratio between front and rear and exactly evenly from side to side. Place heavy items low, light ones high. The design of the bags influences arrangement, but in general, the heavy compact items, such as a stove, fuel bottles, shoes, and tools, should be packed in the bottom of the bags and in the front of the bike. A heavy handlebar bag interferes with the handling of the bike and no more than ten pounds should be carried there.

The volume of my rear panniers is 1770 cubic inches, which is not as large as rear panniers can be. On summer tours, I have plenty of room with my rear panniers and a small handlebar bag. I pack a light sleeping bag and a couple of heavy articles, like a book and a sweater, in one side of the panniers. On the other side I put the rest of my clothes and maybe some oranges or figs. One rear pocket of the panniers carries tools, and the one on the other side carries personal items. On top of the rack I carry my tent rolled up in a pad and both rolled up in a plastic ground cloth. Underneath the straps that hold the tent to the rack, I put my jacket, when I'm not wearing it, and a Big Chief writing tablet. In the handlebar bag is a bowl, spoon, knife, cash, pens, brush, and lots of other little things I use frequently. Food bought during the day is tucked into the handlebar bag, under the flaps of the rear panniers, or into a plastic bag tied to the straps in the rear.

To increase carrying capacity in order to bring a stove and heavier clothes, I use front panniers. Everything heavy is carried there. The stove is strapped onto the front rack. The sleeping bag is moved from inside the rear pannier to the rack and rolled up beside the tent inside plastic. When using front and rear panniers, I don't need a handlebar bag. As food disappears from the front and room becomes available, items from the rear are moved forward.

Above all else, keep your sleeping bag dry. Carry it in a waterproof sack. Panniers should always be seam-sealed and lined with plastic if there is any chance of rain on your route.

A loaded bike handles differently than an unloaded one, and a heavily loaded bike handles differently than a lightly loaded bike. Practice riding your loaded bike on several types of road surface and terrain. Braking takes longer since the inertia of the increased weight pushes you forward. Racks must be securely mounted, and packs must be securely attached to racks. An unstable, poorly balanced load is extremely dangerous going down hill and extremely tiring under any condition.

Keep in mind the number of miles you plan to average each day when reaching for stuff to put in your bags. If you intend to ride 75 to 125 miles a day, you will want to pack much lighter than if you plan on covering 50 miles a day.

After each tour, take inventory of what you brought and determine what you needed more of or what you didn't need at all.

# Timetable

Bill Woolston

Six to nine months ahead is not too far in advance to plan for a bike camping trip lasting a month or two. Most people need that much time. You will need more time to plan for a trip outside the United States and Canada, less if you are a seasoned cycle tourist. Planning to get off work and saving the money for the trip are two preparations that usually take some time.

Simultaneously, you should acquire information about biking and camping, plan your route, develop lists of needs, collect equipment, and ride your bike.

**Acquire information.** The information gathering phase of planning should continue right up to the last moment when you find out the weather report on the day of departure. If you don't have a bike, or a bike that is usable for a long tour, concentrate your effort on purchasing a bike appropriate to you and your purposes. If you are sure you know what you want, it's wise to buy as far ahead as possible before the tour. However, if you're not sure what you want, then perhaps the place to begin is at the library. Check out all the biking books, skim them, and cleave onto one or two readable books to study carefully. Visit bike shops, collect manufacturers' brochures, and study them. Talk to bike owners about their bikes and ride friends' bikes.

If you have a bike you are planning to use, bring it in the house for a few evenings. Examine it with a very discriminating eye enlightened by your recent reading. Count its teeth, measure its tubes. Mentally dissect its wonderfully ingenious

wheels. With a maintenance manual or assembly instruction booklet on your lap, figure out how it was put together and how it works.

You probably had an idea about where you wanted to go when you first imagined yourself bike camping. Begin to plan your route in greater detail. This may involve writing to government agencies, map suppliers, or cycling organizations for information. You may want to subscribe to cycling periodicals or join a national organization that promotes touring (see the References section at the back of this book). A visit to a local bicycle club will open up more sources of information. Browse around camping stores and study catalogs of outdoor suppliers. Ask informed questions of experienced cyclists and campers. The most important result of this information gathering process is that you become able to determine what you need for the tour you have in mind. It will be helpful to...

**Prepare a list of needs.** In the early stages of planning, it is difficult to tell the difference between needs and wants. Later on, perhaps as late as when you are packing, certain things will seem pure indulgences and will be dropped, like pianos along the Oregon Trail. Of course, my needs may be bric-a-brac to you, and to some, a small radio or cassette player is a pure necessity.

A list of needs includes what to do as well as what to have: who to talk and write to, what to buy, borrow, or make. At this point, a little extravagance won't hurt as you...

**Begin to collect.** Set aside a corner someplace and begin tossing stuff into it that you may want to take with you. Put a box on the kitchen counter and start collecting equipment, recipes, and ingredients on slips of paper to remind you what not to forget in the final rush of packing. Check over your tent, panniers, sleeping bag, and rain gear for tears. Make repairs and seal seams, if necessary. Shop around at secondhand stores for practical clothes at practical prices. Shopping well ahead of your departure date will increase your chances of finding good deals. I bought my tent at a bike show and equipment swap held in the city park.

Surely, if slowly, all will be honed down to a definite route and date of departure. While the lists of things to do and to acquire are getting smaller, the pile of equipment in the corner is growing. Now is the time to sift through it again and again, keeping in mind the New England adage: use it up, wear it out; make it do, or do without. During the process of learning, collecting, and sifting, don't forget to...

**Ride your bike.** If you are waiting for the bike you ordered to arrive, don't just sit around. Start training. Ride your old bike or borrow a friend's. When you get your new bike, ride the devil out of it, then take it in for adjustments before you leave. If you do not ride a bike at least every day for 20 minutes, then begin to. If that is impossible, then make a concentrated effort at conditioning a month or two before the trip.

In addition to riding a bike as much as possible, participate in other aerobic exercise such as running, jumping rope, playing soccer or basketball, swimming, or go for vigorous hikes. If you feel you are overweight, perhaps making some dietary changes at the same time is in order.

As the departure date gets close, you may feel frantic, but one way to reduce the possibility of last minute omission is to...

**Have a dress rehearsal.** A few days before leaving, put your black shorts on, pack up all your cares and woe, and get out of town. Pretend it's opening night. After a pleasant 50-mile ride up and down several hills, find a campsite. Set up your tent and fix dinner. Relax. Think. What have I forgotten to do or to acquire? This is the best way to discover the tent stakes are still at home, the stove suddenly doesn't work, or that you have forgotten your camera.

If you are touring with a group, get together to discuss equipment several days before leaving. Everyone does not need to bring the same freewheel remover. Six people don't need six tents, but do need two Frisbees. Take several rides together so each member has a preview of what to expect from the others.

Check over your bike for the ninety-ninth time. Are the tires still in good shape? Any new bruises or cuts? Has the bottom bracket tightened or loosened? Do the hubs and pedals spin freely? Does the freewheel need another shot of oil? Are the brake blocks in top condition? Have the rims maintained their true? Is the shifting flawless? Are you sure you have a low gear low enough, now that you've ridden a packed bike 50 miles? How about the packing system? Is it convenient and neat? Is the weight distributed properly? Take the time to have your home on wheels in perfect order.

**The day before.** Pack everything and as you do, write down the items. Look at the list and ask yourself if you have everything. Film? travelers' checks? can opener? extra spokes? safety pins? dental floss? the just-washed sweater? the borrowed freewheel tool?

You may want to bake some high-energy goodies, such as the sesame crisps suggested in the section on eating. After everything is packed, tuck in some fresh fruit.

**The day of departure.** Eat a hearty breakfast, fill the waterbottle and consciously place it in the carrier, grab your toothbrush, some toilet paper, your sunglasses, and helmet. Check again to make sure your money is on board, not on top of the dresser. Make sure the pump is securely fastened to the frame, the brake quick-releases shut, the tires full, and all pannier straps and closures fastened. Bye, bye!

# THE TOURING BICYCLE

Late one winter, I came down with serious cabin fever. I glowered out the window at a hostile world. My kids performed amazing feats on their secondhand bikes while I got flabby at my desk proofreading. I remembered seeing a bike shop in an alley somewhere. One drizzly day, I went into this dark and oily place. "I want a bike," I said to the bearded man with stained fingers, and I stood as tall as possible in my cowboy boots.

The man leaned across the counter and said in a lowered voice that he could even make me a deal, since it was winter, as long as I didn't care if the bike was orange. Seeing that I didn't flinch, he began to promote the orange arrangement hanging like a bat on the ceiling above me. I could have been in a Moroccan bazaar, so unfamiliar was I with my surroundings, so little did I follow his narrative. I slapped down a twenty dollar bill and said I would see him again next week.

Hard enough to pay for, it was harder yet to ride. I made all the classic falls, such as tipping over at a stoplight with my feet stuck in the toe clips and laying down in gravel after attempting a sharp turn. Winter came again, and it never occurred to me to ride. I retired the bike to the garage. But while it snowed, fantasies simmered. An image of two cyclists I had passed quickly in my car a year earlier was superimposed on my light table and typewriter. I saw their lithe bodies and pleased faces. Why not me? I had nothing to lose but my cellulite. Come August, I decided I would ride down to New Mexico and visit my folks. It's all downhill, south is, isn't it?

The frame was made of medium-carbon, straight-gauge tubing. The wheels had alloy rims and quick-release hubs. The crankset was alloy and cotterless. Derailleurs and brakes were the inexpensive models of well-known names. The geometry tended toward the racing style rather than touring. I put on a "granny" gear, handlebar padding, a women's touring saddle, and heavy-duty tires. I went over the bike with a mechanic a few days before I left. The only trouble I had in 1550 miles was one flat tire and two broken spokes. By the end of the trip, everything needed cleaning and adjusting, but I was perfectly satisfied with the bike's performance. I didn't know enough not to be satisfied.

Bitten by the touring bug, I sold the bike and bought a more expensive chrome-moly, double-butted frame. For the educational value, I built up the bike myself under the tutelage of my roommate who worked as a bike mechanic. All the choices of parts were made, not after methodically considering the alternatives, but after seeing what was locally available at a price I was willing to pay. I made a blatant mistake—the frame is too large—and I made other choices that I now regret. I would like to try non-parallel head and seat tube angles. I would like to have more gears than the seven usable ones I have now. Nevertheless, the bike is reliable and will give me thousands more miles of enjoyment, adventure, and just plain transportation.

# Which Bike

Whether it is a one-speed with baskets, kickstand, wide tires and trailer, or a skinny, nimble fifteen-speed, a bike is a simple and efficient machine. Most people would prefer not to tour for long on an old, utilitarian clunker, but it is possible to arrive at a great number of places on a great variety of two-wheeled, unmotorized vehicles. If part of the purpose of the trip is enjoyment, however, it behooves the cycle tourist to keep in mind two truisms about equipment: there is no substitute for quality, and nothing so pleases as having the right thing at the right time.

If you own one of the millions of ten-speeds in general use, take a hard look at it before you take it touring. If the frame is too big for you or is out of alignment, if the rims are steel, the components showing wear, and the total weight is around 30 or 35 pounds, consider buying a new bike.

If your old one exhausts you, how can you enjoy touring? So much time will be spent worrying, making repairs, or riding

slowly out of fear, that you'll wish you had never gotten the crazy notion in your head.

However, if the frame fits and is straight and has good quality wheels and components, then there is little reason to start all over. Some changes, such as in gearing, might be wise. Using a leather saddle or one designed for touring, fenders, and handlebar padding will result in a bike that is more appropriate for long-distance touring. With new, adjusted bearings, new cables and brake blocks, and wheels that are new or rebuilt, your old bike will be full of new life. The frame can even be repainted.

Old or new, tour on a bike you'll enjoy riding day after day because it is comfortable, stable, dependable—and fast.

# New Bikes

Buy from a professional bike dealer. The chances are greater that the bike will be properly assembled, which is usually not the case with department store and discount house bikes. A local shop can guarantee and service what it sells and may offer a couple of free tune-ups on a new bike. Usually, the shop owner/-mechanic is also a cyclist and will know and care about proper fitting. You can learn a lot from such a person.

The beginning cyclist who goes to buy a bicycle for touring will probably be offered a multi-purpose ten-speed. This common bicycle, manufactured for the average person, should be altered to provide the most satisfying touring. You will probably have to buy a different saddle (leather or touring) to insure comfort and change the gearing to achieve a low of 30 inches. Make sure the pedals can take toe clips, that the rims are alloy and, most of all, that the bike fits.

It is easy to spend $1000 before you have your new bike home and $1000 more before you leave on tour. It would be difficult to spend less than $275. There are many fine choices between $300 and $500. At some point, a lot of money is traded for fewer grams or prestigious names. Awareness of weight is a reasonable concern, and reputations for high quality are usually deserved, but most tourists think in pounds or kilograms, not grams, and are more interested in good times than the names on their bikes.

On the other hand, when you can pick up (with one hand) your transportation and everything you will need on tour, who cares if it costs filthy lucre? Think of what you have spent, and possibly do spend, on your automobile.

Be a knowledgeable consumer. Of course, there are shops where selling bikes is more important than selling the right bike to a customer. Try to have some idea of what you want when you walk in the shop, but don't have your mind irrevocably set. Learn the names of the bicycle parts so that when the salesperson says "quick-release hubs," you will know he or she is talking about wheels. It keeps the shop owner honest when a customer gets down on his knees and fiddles with the cranks, as long as the customer knows what to fiddle for.

Usually, the first thing a customer does when examining a bike is to squeeze the brake levers. Naturally, bike sellers prepare for this and adjust the brakes to feel desirably tight. Demonstrate to the salesperson that you are a knowledgeable consumer. Check the relationship of the brake pads to the rims. They should make contact just slightly below the edge of the rim and should be slightly toed-in so the forward edge of the pad contacts the rim first. The brake arms should reach evenly for the rim and rest after braking at an equal distance from the rim.

Spin the wheels. If the hubs are properly adjusted, the wheels will rotate smoothly but will not have any side-to-side play. The weight of the valve stem

and stop gradually, not with a little jerk. Hold the crank and chainstay tube beside each other with one hand and gently push and pull on the crank, checking for side-to-side play. There shouldn't be any.

If you want to check frame alignment, tie a string on one rear dropout, go around the head tube, and tie it to the other side of the rear dropout in the same position. Measure the distance between the string and the seat tube on both sides. It should be exactly the same.

Unless you are an experienced rider, the shop may not allow a test ride. If you do test ride, shift through all gears.

If you think you might want to revise the gearing, make sure the crankset will allow changing chainrings. A reputable dealer won't mind gear changes—freewheels, chainrings, or even a whole crankset—with price adjustments. Many riders would do well to change the chainrings from the usual 52/40 to 50/36, whether they plan to tour or not. The smaller chainrings give lower gears and encourage better pedaling habits. Remember that if you change the size of the chainring and cogs, you may have to change the derailleurs, too. If you think you will ever ride in the rain, make sure that fenders will fit on the frame.

You may want to invest in a custom bike, made specifically for you. There are many excellent frame builders. A local bike shop will usually be able to supply information and addresses, as will bicycling magazines.

should pull the wheel around so the valve stops at the bottom of the rotation. This test won't work if the wheel has spoke reflectors on it. The spokes should be evenly taut, and spoke threads shouldn't show below the nipple. The rims should be true and centered over the axles.

Pedals should spin smoothly. To be generally useful for touring, the pedals should accept toe clips. To check the bottom bracket adjustment, take the chain off the chainring and lay it on the bottom bracket lug. The crank should spin easily

# Fitting

Bill Woolston

It is extremely important that the bike and rider fit each other. Most bikes are designed to appeal to a wide and general audience. If the frame fits, the rest of the bike can be customized to the individual. In addition, while proper adjustment is crucial, the body will accommodate a less-than-ideal fit and make the best of it. There are limits for safety and comfort, of course, but they are highly individual.

Begin by making sure that when you straddle the top tube, there is at least an inch between you and the cold hard metal. If there isn't, go down to the next size. A frame that is too big is dangerous, weighs more, and is less rigid than a smaller one. Tourists can use a larger frame than racers, but the smallest frame that fits is the best choice.

If a suitable 19-inch diamond frame can't be found, buy a mixte design. If you have to jump off the saddle quickly, you will appreciate the top tube not being there. The mixte has two tubes that slant from the headset to the rearstays. A high-quality mixte frame is acceptable for touring. Frames should be bought that fit the anatomy, not fashion.

There are three places where your body and bike meet. The goal in setting up your bike is to establish a happy relationship between you and the saddle, the pedals, and the handlebars.

Saddle position can be varied by moving it up and down, forward and back, and tilting it toward or away from the handlebars. Saddle height (limited by frame size), can be set by taking 105 to 109 percent of the length of the inside of the leg from floor to crotch. Measure, and set the saddle at that height by measuring from the top of the saddle down the seat tube to the center of the pedal spindle with the crank in its fullest extension.

You can also position the saddle just by what feels comfortable. Sit on the bike with someone holding it steady. If the saddle is too high, your hips will rock when you pedal backwards with your heels on the pedals. Make sure there is a slight bend in your knees when your heel is on the pedal at the bottom of a stroke.

Within the limitations of the seat tube angle, you can adjust your position over the frame by moving the saddle forward or back. What you want is the center of the knee directly over the center of the pedal when the cranks are horizontal. The ball of the foot should be directly over the center of the pedal as well. The tip of the seat should be behind the center of the bottom bracket.

Many people like the front of the saddle slightly higher than the rear because the body weight is back toward the hip bones and somewhat off the crotch. If the saddle is tilted down too far in front, it is a fight to stay on the seat. Wrists become sore and fingers numb from pressure. Women often prefer the saddle lower in the front than men do because their genitals are crushed against the front of the

saddle, especially when riding on the turned-down part of the handlebars. Start with a level saddle and make adjustments later.

Handlebars can be raised or lowered and held at various distances away from you by changing the height of the stem. Typically, the handlebars are set a couple of inches below the level of the seat. A tourist will generally want a more upright position than a racer, so the handlebars are set higher, and may even be level with the seat. For safety, there must be 2 1/2 inches of stem remaining in the head tube. Make sure that the stem is not too short. A stem extension that is too long causes neck and shoulder aches and prevents the proper distrubution of weight on the bike. With hands on the drops, a line from the rider's nose should fall directly to the handlebars.

After you think you have the bike set up properly, ride a hundred miles or so, then make some changes and note the effects. Minor changes in saddle height, tilt, and handlebar height can have great impact on pedaling efficiency and comfort. Some changes of position on the bike will be desired as experience is accumulated.

When touring, take with you the tools necessary to change saddle position. Varying the saddle position will help you learn what works best for you and may relieve discomfort resulting from day-after-day riding.

# FRAMES

The standard frame style for touring bikes is the diamond frame, consisting of a top tube, seat tube, down tube, and head tube, seatstay, chainstay, fork, and usually various lugs including the bottom bracket. The fork is separate, but the fork and frame function as a unit, and together they are the soul of your bike.

The weight of a bare frame is a rough guide to its quality, but workmanship in fitting the tubes together is more important. Tubes are joined either with or without lugs. A lug acts as a sleeve over the joint and reinforces the area. Most touring bikes have lugged joints. The strength of a joint depends upon how well the parts fit together and the skill of the person who brazes them. Brazing is a process of joining tubes using a filler metal that has a melting point much below that of the tube material. The filler flows between the lug and the tube and bonds them. High heat must be avoided during assembly because it weakens a lightweight tube. Look for good lug work. The joint should appear clean.

The tubes have to be aligned so the bicycle tracks properly. A frame is aligned if it can be divided into two exact, symmetrical halves by a centerline straight through the frame. Tracking means simply that the rear wheel follows the line, or track, of the front wheel. Track is also a function of properly built wheels.

Terms used to describe frame material and quality can be very confusing. Low-carbon steel is weak in comparision to the finer alloys. Therefore, the walls of tubing made from it must be thicker. Also, low-carbon tubes have a seam and are assembled by high-heat welding. The frame that results from welded tubes (pipes) is heavy, sturdy, and intended for utility use.

The minimum specifications for a touring bike should be a seamless tube frame of medium-carbon steel. A frame of 1018 or 1020 steel (18 and 20 percent carbon, respectively) has probably been assembled by brazing. A frame that has been tempered has been uniformly cooled in a bath which restores the desirable springiness the tubing had before it was heated in the assembly process.

High-quality bicycle tubing is made

from high-carbon, chromium-molybdenum or manganese-molybdenum steel. A frame designated "4130" is high-carbon, "chrome-moly." The cold-drawn seamless tubes are very strong, and consequently thick-walled and light. Five pages of this book (.56 mm), approximate the thickness of the wall in the center of a manganese-molybdenum top tube which is similar in performance to chrome-moly. A frame of such alloys is responsive and resilient, that is, it can flex and readily return to its original shape.

Butting is a process in which the walls of a tube at the ends are thickened without increasing the outside diameter of the tube. The strength of the ends of the tubes, where the joints are made, is increased. Double-butted tubing is thicker at both ends.

The fork consists of a steering column, crown, blades, and ends. The handling characteristics of a bike are greatly influenced by the design of the fork. The fork must be able to absorb shock, yet provide sensitive steering.

# Geometry

The angles and dimensions of a frame are called its geometry. They vary according to the intended use of the bike. If you buy a custom bike the frame will be made to your size and cycling style.

Frame size is measured from the center of the bottom bracket to the top of the seat lug.

Top tube length is measured from the center of the head tube to the center of the seat tube. It affects the overall balance of the rider's weight on the frame.

Chainstay length is measured from the center of the rear wheel axle to the center of the bottom bracket spindle. It affects the distribution of the rider's weight by changing the position of the rear wheel in relation to the rest of the bike. Chainstay length for a touring bike is often between 17 and 17 1/2 inches. A shorter length makes the frame stiffer and more responsive.

Head tube angle is measured between the front of the head tube and an imaginary intersecting line parallel to the ground. If the top tube is parallel to the floor, imagine an extension of the top tube. For touring bikes, the angle is usually 72 or 73 degrees.

Seat tube angle is measured between the front of the seat tube and an imaginary line parallel to the ground. This angle is usually 72 or 73 degrees for a touring bike. The seat tube and the head tube do not have to be parallel. The seat tube angle affects the distribution of the rider's weight on the frame. The tourist on "shallow angles" is positioned further back on the bike than the racer on "steeper angles" and enjoys a more comfortable ride. Steeper angles provide quicker handling than shallow angles.

Fork rake is the amount of bend in the fork measured perpendicularly between a line drawn through the center of the axle that's parallel to a line through the center of the headset bearings. Racing bikes have a short rake, from 1 1/2 to 1 3/4 inches, which gives a harsh ride but very responsive steering. The longer rake of a touring bike, up to two inches, gives a more comfortable ride at the expense of quick steering. However, quick steering on a bicycle loaded with touring equipment is not necessarily an advantage and could

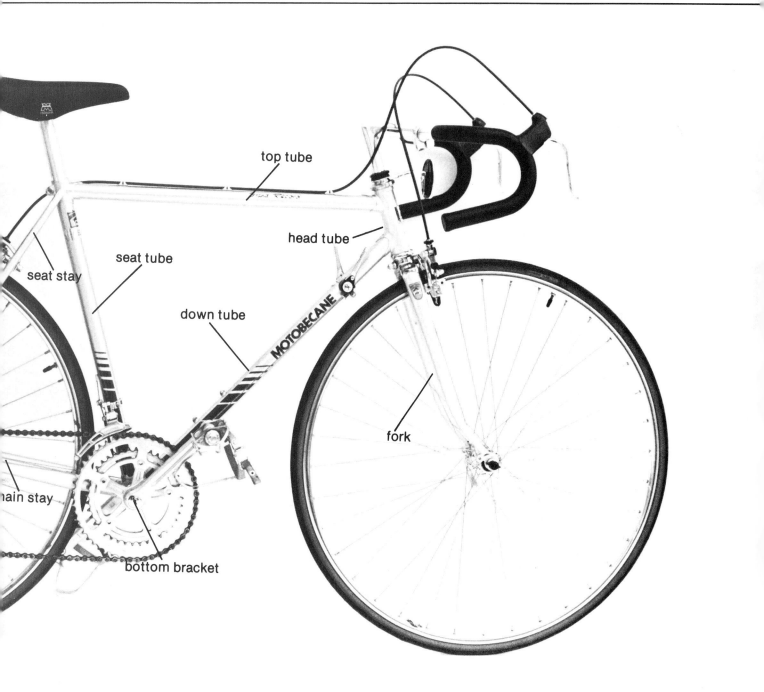

cause an accident. A longer rake means the bike will self-steer somewhat, which is safer. The weight of front panniers will dampen the ride, making it possible to have a rake on the short side without sacrificing too much comfort.

Trail is the distance between a line drawn down through the center of the head tube to the ground and a vertical line from the front axle to the ground. Trail is a function of head tube angle and fork rake. Stability increases as trail increases.

Drop is measured from the center of the bottom bracket to an imaginary horizontal line above the bottom bracket drawn between the centers of the two wheel axles. The greater the drop, the lower the center of gravity, which increases stability. Past a certain point, the pedals might hit the ground when cornering.

Ideally, a frame would be stiff enough to transmit all the energy applied on the pedals to the rear wheel, yet be flexible enough to provide a comfortable ride. "Compromise is what frame design is all about," says Sam Braxton, noted frame builder. A racer wants stiffness and responsiveness, whereas a tourist is concerned with comfort and stability. Bicycles with shallow angles generally have fairly long wheelbases (the distance between the front and rear axles) of 40 inches or more. They are more flexible than bikes with steep angles and a short (38-inch) wheel base. The latter is faster but tiresome to ride for long periods of time.

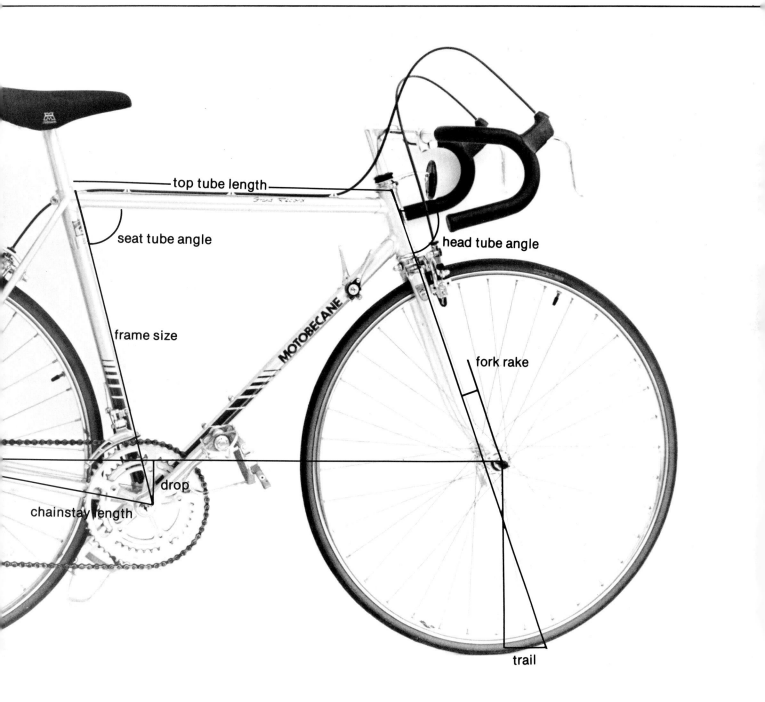

top tube length

seat tube angle

head tube angle

frame size

fork rake

MOTOBECANE

drop

chainstay length

trail

# WHEELS

If the frame is the soul of the bike, the wheels, with their hubs, spokes, rims, and tires, are its heart. Choice of wheels is a fundamental consideration. What you want are the lightest wheels which are strong enough to carry the heaviest loads on the roughest roads that you anticipate.

# Hubs

The flange is the part of the hub to which the spokes are attached. Variations in flange size create different riding characteristics of the wheel. The flange size, spoking pattern, and the spoke length are important variables of wheel feel. Both low-flange, four-cross, and high flange, three-cross are suitable for touring bikes. But some people prefer the high-flange, three-cross because the ride is a little stiffer.

Sealed bearing hubs are difficult for dirt or people to enter, and they need less maintenance than regular (unsealed), hubs. All hubs will eventually get dirty, but sealed ones keep cleaner longer. They may offer less rolling resistance as well. However, many people want to adjust the tolerances themselves and control the cleaning and packing of the bearings. Sealed bearing hubs usually have to be sent to the factory for cleaning and repairs. A properly adjusted, unsealed hub of professional quality will roll as well, and possibly better, than a sealed one. Don't take on world tours any sealed hubs or bottom brackets which you can't service yourself or get fixed easily.

A quick-release hub has a hollow axle which contains a skewer and clamp that hold the wheel in the frame dropouts. The alternative is a hub with a solid axle, which uses a nut to secure the wheel to the frame. With a quick-release hub, the wheel can quickly be taken off the frame. Changing a flat and loading the bike into a car is easier, but so is wheel theft. When locking a bike with quick-release hubs, lock the wheels to the frame.

# Spokes

Spokes are made in different lengths, thicknesses, materials, and shapes. Fourteen-gauge spokes are a good choice for large riders or heavy loads. The higher the gauge number, the thinner the spoke. Double-butted spokes are lighter and more flexible than straight gauge spokes and strong enough for a light rider. The longer the spoke and the more crosses it makes to the rim, the more shock-absorbent, stronger, and heavier the wheel. The shorter the spoke and the fewer crosses it makes, the stiffer, more responsive, and lighter the wheel. A four-cross rear wheel has greater ability to withstand pedaling force than a three-cross wheel.

Most hubs, and thus rims, have 36 holes. The number of spokes affects the strength and weight of the wheel. Occasionally, a 40-spoke rear wheel will be used for touring by a heavy rider. Tandems may have 48 spokes. The most important factor of wheel strength, however, is quality wheel building that results in a true, round wheel with even tension on all the spokes. The spoke is tensioned with a nut called a nipple. Broken spokes, the bane of cycle touring, don't necessarily have to happen. A spoke seldom breaks on a well-built wheel.

# Rims

The weight of a rim (and tire) is especially important. When the rim is moving, its weight rotates at a distance from the hub, on the circumference of the wheel. A rotating wheel on an accelerating or decelerating bike has both circular momentum and straight-ahead momentum. One pound on the rim is worth about 2.8 pounds on the frame when starting or stopping. The heavier the wheels, the greater the inhibitory effect. More energy is then required to set the wheels in motion and to stop the motion.

Therefore, light alloy rims are more satisfactory for touring than heavy steel ones, except for heavy loads on bad roads. However, the best rim of any material and design is the one that is manufactured in a perfect circle to begin with.

Rims are designed to accommodate either wired-on tires or tubular tires. Wired-ons need a channel in the rim. The tire is held onto the rim by a wire bead in the tire and by tire pressure. A tubular tire must be on a tubular rim. The tubular rim/tire combination is lighter than the wired-on combination, but is not generally recommended for touring. A very narrow rim has limited applicability for touring.

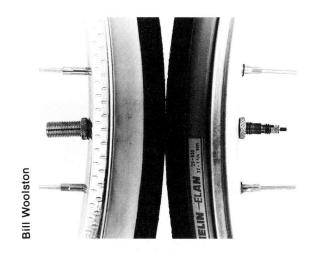

Bill Woolston

# Tires

In tires, as in rims, the "best" is the lightest tire that carries the load. There are two types of tires and both are used for touring. Wired-ons, also called clinchers, are preferable to tubulars, also called sew-ups. Wired-ons are cheaper, easier to repair and more available in the United States and Canada. They are usually wider and more sure-footed. Lightweight wired-ons narrow as tubulars are available, but the standard size for touring is the 27-inch by 1 1/4-inch (rather than 1-inch or 1 1/8-inch), or the slightly smaller 700c by 32mm (rather than 28mm or 30mm), particularly in the rear. For a properly divided load with 40 percent of the weight up front, a wider, and thus heavier, tire is not needed, especially if the rider is lightweight and careful. The narrower a tire is, however, the more likely it is to be deflected by gravel or holes in the road, resulting in loss of control. In hot, gooey pavement or on dirt roads, the narrower tire bogs down more readily.

Tire selection also depends upon the rim size. A 27-inch tire is not interchangeable with a 700c tire on the same rim. The same frame, however, can accommodate both rim sizes.

Tubes have two styles of valves: Schrader and Presta. Presta valves weigh less, and a tube with a Presta valve is easier to pump up. Unless an adaptor is used, the same pump cannot fit both valves. A frame-fit pump is elegant in design. The pump size is proportionate to the size of the frame, and therefore, the rider. It attaches neatly onto the seat tube.

Schrader valves are identical to auto tire valves, and a tube with a Schrader valve can be filled by a service station air hose. In order to avoid a blowout or damaged tube, fill the tube with short bursts of air. Use a bike pressure gauge to measure pressure. It is important to keep tires inflated to their maximum pressure, usually between 90 and 100 pounds for the lighter touring tires. The pressure in the rear tire can be increased by 10 pounds or so when carrying a heavy rider or load. It can be reduced slightly for improved traction on dirt roads.

Rolling resistance contributes to the loss of pedaling energy. It can be reduced by keeping tires inflated to their maximum, oiling and adjusting bearings, maintaining proper weight balance, and riding on the smoothest part of the highway.

# GEARING

The French velocipede, a predecessor of the modern bicycle, had cranks with pedals attached directly to the hub of the front wheel, as a child's tricycle does today. One revolution of the pedals advanced the machine a distance equal to the circumference of the front wheel, maybe ten feet.

The English high-wheeler was designed to increase the distance traveled in a given time by using a front wheel that was as large as could possibly be straddled and pedaled. The larger the front wheel, the further the cyclist could go for each revolution of the pedals, but the greater the effort. The diameter of the high-wheeler front wheel was as much as 60 inches. Consequently, they were difficult to mount, balance, and ride downhill. The long-legged, gigantic, and fearless cyclists ruled the roost.

In 1879, the chain-and-sprocket drive to the rear wheel was developed and the result was the "safety" bike. A chain-and-sprocket system makes the wheels turn faster than the pedals. The various sprocket sizes supply different gears. The wheels can then be a convenient mounting height of 26 or 27 inches in diameter.

# Ten-Speeds

Changing the gears on a ten-speed bike, with its two chainrings in front and five cogs in the rear, is like changing the diameter of its rear, or driving, wheel. Bicyclists still talk about their gears as "inches." To find out your bike's "wheel sizes," count the teeth on all the sprockets (front chainrings and rear cogs), and write the numbers like this:

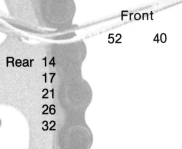

|      | Front |    |
|------|-------|----|
|      | 52    | 40 |
| Rear 14 |    |    |
| 17   |       |    |
| 21   |       |    |
| 26   |       |    |
| 32   |       |    |

Then, using the gear chart, fill in the gear numbers. These numbers are obtained by dividing chainring size by cog size and multiplying the result by wheel diameter. In the example above, which is the gearing on my first bike when I bought it, 52 divided by 14 multiplied by 27 equals 100.3. The results for all the gears are:

|    | 52    | 40   |
|----|-------|------|
| 14 | 100.3 | 77.1 |
| 17 | 82.6  | 63.5 |
| 21 | 66.9  | 51.4 |
| 26 | 54.0  | 41.5 |
| 32 | 43.9  | 33.7 |

The 100.3 number represents how many inches in diameter a wheel would have to be to move a high-wheeler with direct drive the same distance as one revolution of the pedals does a ten-speed in the high gear of this example. In high gear, the chain is on the 52-tooth chainring and the 14-tooth cog and the bike will move forward 314.9 inches (100.3 x pi) with one revolution of the pedals.

Now you know. The knowledge is mind-expanding, even though it's not something you will use as often as a tire lever.

Arrange the above numbers sequentially. Low gear is 33.7. The 43.9 gear should not be used because the chain must deflect too much, causing friction and wear, to reach from the large, outer chainring to the large, inner rear cog. The 51.4 and 54.0 are essentially one gear. The 63.5 and the 66.9 are very close. The 77.1, in which the chain reaches from the small (inner) chainring to the small (outer) rear cog, can be used even though the chain must deflect quite a bit. In reality, therefore, I had six, maybe seven, usable gears. I wanted a lower gear for touring, so I changed the small chainring to a 36-tooth sprocket and got two gears in the 30s: 37.4 and a low gear of 30.4.

On my next bike, I put a 52/36 arrangement on the front and a 13/16/20/24/28 cluster on the rear, giving me a low of 34.8 and a high of 108 and demonstrating a poor choice of gearing. Since my new frame was lighter than my old one and had lighter components, I figured overall weight reduction would balance out the overall higher gears. I had seven, maybe eight, usable gears, but I so rarely used the 108 high that it was a waste of gearing space. After going over Teton Pass in Wyoming, a ten percent grade, I vowed never again to be without a 30-inch low gear. For me, a high gear over 100 is silly and a low gear of 30 is necessary. I changed the chainrings to 50/36 and the freewheel to 14/17/21/26/32. For stronger riders or a flat terrain, a 52/38 with 14/17/20/24/28 provides a smooth progression of gears. A 44/32 in the front and a 12 to 28 in the rear gives a high of 99 and low of 31. Smaller sprockets all around mean less weight. Shifting is easier. The disadvantages are that small

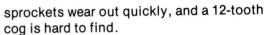

sprockets wear out quickly, and a 12-tooth cog is hard to find.

Many new bikes have badly selected gear arrangements. Good gearing does not necessarily cost more than bad gearing. If you want to change your gears, first determine the lowest and highest gears you need. Then choose the rest of the gears to give a smooth progression without large jumps between gears, particularly in the middle of the gearing range where most of the pedaling is done. The most common arrangements on stock bicycles are a 52/40 front with either a 14/17/21/26/32 or 14/17/20/24/28 rear. If the front chainrings are changed to something like 50/38 or 50/36, the entire range of gears is moved downward, a better place for most cyclists to be.

Beginning cyclists almost always pedal in too high a gear. Using a high gear seems like a good idea because you move so far in just one pedal revolution. But pushing that high gear and pedaling at a relatively slow rate soon becomes very tiring. The solution is simple: just pedal in a lower gear and pedal faster.

# Ten-Speed Shifting

Shifting through the gears consecutively usually requires a double shift, changing both the front and rear position of the chain, in order to get the next gear. I like to avoid double shifting, but that means I must skip a precious gear or two. It is a good idea to study the shifting pattern of your gearing system or one you are considering obtaining.

Even though double shifting may be a nuisance, it's best to use as many gears as possible. The smoothest and most gradual transitions result in the most efficient pedaling.

Write your gear numbers with shifting sequence on a card and tape it to the handlebars so that when you are riding, you will learn how "64 inches" feels to pedal. Translating feel into numbers will supply you with a language for understanding gears. Memorize your shifting pattern and stick to it.

# Gear Chart for 27-inch Wheels

**number of teeth on front chainring**

| | | 24 | 26 | 28 | 30 | 32 | 34 | 36 | 38 | 40 | 42 | 44 | 45 | 46 | 47 | 48 | 49 | 50 | 52 | 53 | 54 | 55 | 56 |
|---|---|---|---|---|---|---|---|---|---|---|---|---|---|---|---|---|---|---|---|---|---|---|---|
| | 12 | 54.0 | 58.5 | 63.0 | 67.5 | 72.0 | 76.5 | 81.0 | 85.5 | 90.0 | 94.5 | 99.0 | 101.2 | 103.5 | 105.7 | 108.0 | 110.2 | 112.3 | 117.0 | 119.3 | 121.5 | 122.7 | 126.0 |
| | 13 | 49.8 | 54.0 | 58.1 | 62.3 | 66.4 | 70.6 | 74.7 | 78.9 | 83.1 | 87.2 | 91.4 | 93.4 | 95.5 | 97.6 | 99.7 | 101.8 | 103.9 | 108.0 | 110.0 | 112.1 | 114.2 | 116.3 |
| | 14 | 46.2 | 50.1 | 54.0 | 57.8 | 61.7 | 65.5 | 69.5 | 73.3 | 77.1 | 81.0 | 84.9 | 86.7 | 88.7 | 90.6 | 92.6 | 94.5 | 96.4 | 100.3 | 102.2 | 104.1 | 106.0 | 108.0 |
| | 15 | 43.2 | 46.8 | 50.4 | 54.0 | 57.6 | 61.1 | 64.8 | 68.4 | 72.0 | 75.6 | 79.2 | 81.0 | 82.8 | 84.6 | 86.4 | 88.2 | 90.0 | 93.6 | 95.4 | 97.2 | 99.0 | 100.8 |
| | 16 | 40.5 | 43.7 | 47.2 | 50.6 | 54.0 | 57.2 | 60.9 | 64.1 | 67.5 | 70.9 | 74.3 | 76.0 | 77.6 | 79.3 | 81.0 | 82.7 | 84.4 | 87.8 | 89.4 | 91.1 | 92.8 | 94.5 |
| | 17 | 38.1 | 41.2 | 44.4 | 47.6 | 50.8 | 54.0 | 57.2 | 60.3 | 63.5 | 66.7 | 69.9 | 71.5 | 73.1 | 74.6 | 76.2 | 77.8 | 79.4 | 82.6 | 84.1 | 85.7 | 87.3 | 88.9 |
| | 18 | 36.0 | 39.0 | 42.0 | 45.0 | 48.0 | 51.0 | 54.0 | 57.0 | 60.0 | 63.0 | 66.0 | 67.5 | 69.0 | 70.5 | 72.0 | 73.5 | 75.0 | 78.0 | 79.5 | 81.0 | 82.5 | 84.0 |
| | 19 | 34.1 | 36.8 | 39.7 | 42.6 | 45.5 | 48.2 | 51.1 | 54.0 | 56.8 | 59.7 | 62.5 | 64.0 | 65.4 | 66.8 | 68.2 | 69.6 | 71.1 | 73.9 | 75.3 | 76.7 | 78.1 | 79.5 |
| | 20 | 32.4 | 35.1 | 37.8 | 40.5 | 43.2 | 45.9 | 48.7 | 51.3 | 54.0 | 56.7 | 59.4 | 60.8 | 62.1 | 63.4 | 64.8 | 66.2 | 67.5 | 70.2 | 71.5 | 72.9 | 74.5 | 75.6 |
| | 21 | 30.1 | 33.4 | 36.0 | 38.6 | 41.1 | 43.7 | 46.4 | 48.9 | 51.4 | 54.0 | 56.6 | 57.9 | 59.1 | 60.4 | 61.7 | 63.0 | 64.3 | 66.9 | 68.1 | 69.4 | 70.7 | 72.0 |
| | 22 | 29.4 | 31.9 | 34.3 | 36.8 | 39.2 | 41.6 | 44.2 | 46.6 | 49.1 | 51.5 | 54.0 | 55.2 | 56.1 | 57.6 | 58.9 | 60.1 | 61.4 | 63.8 | 64.0 | 66.2 | 67.5 | 68.7 |
| | 23 | 28.1 | 30.5 | 32.8 | 35.2 | 37.5 | 39.9 | 42.4 | 44.6 | 47.0 | 49.3 | 51.6 | 52.8 | 54.0 | 55.2 | 56.3 | 57.5 | 58.7 | 61.0 | 62.2 | 63.6 | 64.5 | 65.7 |
| | 24 | 27.0 | 29.2 | 31.5 | 33.7 | 36.0 | 38.2 | 40.5 | 42.8 | 45.0 | 47.3 | 49.5 | 50.7 | 51.8 | 52.9 | 54.0 | 55.1 | 56.3 | 58.6 | 59.6 | 60.7 | 61.8 | 63.0 |
| | 25 | 25.9 | 28.0 | 30.2 | 32.4 | 34.6 | 36.7 | 38.9 | 41.0 | 43.2 | 45.4 | 47.5 | 48.6 | 49.7 | 50.8 | 51.8 | 52.9 | 54.0 | 56.2 | 57.2 | 58.3 | 59.4 | 60.4 |
| | 26 | 24.9 | 27.0 | 29.0 | 31.2 | 33.2 | 35.3 | 37.4 | 39.5 | 41.5 | 43.6 | 45.7 | 46.7 | 47.8 | 48.8 | 49.9 | 50.9 | 51.9 | 54.0 | 55.0 | 56.0 | 57.1 | 58.1 |
| | 27 | 24.0 | 26.0 | 28.0 | 30.0 | 32.0 | 34.0 | 36.0 | 38.0 | 40.0 | 42.0 | 44.0 | 45.0 | 46.0 | 47.0 | 48.0 | 49.0 | 50.0 | 52.0 | 53.0 | 54.0 | 55.0 | 56.0 |
| | 28 | 23.1 | 25.0 | 27.0 | 28.9 | 30.8 | 32.8 | 34.8 | 36.6 | 38.6 | 40.5 | 42.4 | 43.4 | 44.4 | 45.3 | 46.3 | 47.2 | 48.2 | 50.1 | 51.1 | 52.0 | 53.0 | 54.0 |
| | 29 | 22.4 | 24.2 | 26.1 | 28.0 | 29.8 | 31.6 | 33.5 | 35.4 | 37.2 | 39.0 | 41.0 | 41.9 | 42.0 | 43.8 | 44.7 | 45.6 | 46.5 | 48.4 | 49.4 | 50.3 | 51.2 | 52.1 |
| | 30 | 21.6 | 23.4 | 25.2 | 27.0 | 28.8 | 30.6 | 32.4 | 34.2 | 36.0 | 37.8 | 39.6 | 40.5 | 41.4 | 42.3 | 43.2 | 44.1 | 45.0 | 46.4 | 47.7 | 48.6 | 49.5 | 50.4 |
| | 31 | 20.9 | 22.6 | 24.4 | 26.2 | 27.9 | 29.6 | 31.4 | 33.1 | 34.8 | 36.6 | 38.3 | 39.2 | 40.1 | 41.0 | 41.8 | 42.6 | 43.5 | 45.2 | 46.2 | 47.0 | 47.9 | 48.8 |
| | 32 | 20.3 | 22.0 | 23.6 | 25.3 | 27.0 | 28.7 | 30.4 | 32.1 | 33.7 | 35.4 | 37.2 | 38.0 | 38.8 | 39.7 | 40.5 | 41.4 | 42.2 | 43.9 | 44.7 | 45.5 | 46.4 | 47.3 |
| | 33 | 19.6 | 21.3 | 22.9 | 24.6 | 26.2 | 27.8 | 29.5 | 31.1 | 32.7 | 34.4 | 36.0 | 36.8 | 37.6 | 38.5 | 39.3 | 40.1 | 40.9 | 42.6 | 43.4 | 44.2 | 45.0 | 45.9 |
| | 34 | 19.1 | 20.6 | 22.2 | 23.8 | 25.4 | 27.0 | 28.6 | 30.2 | 31.8 | 33.3 | 35.0 | 35.7 | 36.5 | 37.4 | 38.1 | 38.9 | 39.7 | 41.3 | 42.1 | 42.9 | 43.6 | 44.4 |

*number of teeth on rear cog*

Below are my gear numbers with the shifting sequence indicated:

|    | 50      | 36      |
|----|---------|---------|
| 14 | 96.4[8] | 69.5    |
| 17 | 79.4[7] | 57.2[5] |
| 21 | 64.3[6] | 46.4[3] |
| 26 | 51.9[4] | 37.4[2] |
| 32 | 42.2    | 30.4[1] |

1. Start at 30.4.
2. First shift, from 30.4 to 37.4, requires that the chain be dropped in the rear from the 32-tooth cog down to the 26-tooth cog. The chain remains on the small chainring.
3. The next gear, 46.4, is reached by changing only the rear position of the chain.
4. In the next change, to 51.9, the chain has to be moved back a cog in the rear and from the small to the large chainring in the front.
5,6. The next gear requires that the chain go back to the small chainring and down two cogs in the rear. I may skip this gear, 57.2, and just go from the 51.9. to the 64.3. Or I may skip two gears and go from the 46.4 to the 64.3, which is an abominable jump of 18 inches.
7,8. From 64.3 to high gear it is a simple matter of changing only the rear position, leaving the chain on the large chainring in the front and dropping down to the smallest cog in the rear.

# Twelve-Speeds

Twelve-speed bikes have a reputation for causing wheel trouble because the rear wheel, with the common six-cog hub, is inherently weaker than a wheel with a five-cog freewheel. In order to center any rear wheel over the axle, the spokes on the freewheel side of the hub have to be more vertical, carry more tension, and are usually shorter than the spokes on the other side. Therefore, they break easier. The common six-cog freewheel, being wider than a five-cog freewheel, requires a rim that is even more deeply dished. Several "close-clearance" six-cog and even seven-cog freewheels are now available. They eliminate the dishing problems that have plagued twelve-speed owners, and, in fact, offer a stronger wheel than the five-cog system.

The additional cog can provide an easier shift sequence or closer steps between gears. The 52/36 chainring, with a 14/16/18/21/26/31 cluster, is a good arrangement, giving a 31-inch low gear.

# Fifteen-Speeds

A fifteen-speed bike has a third chainring and a slightly longer spindle which adds about three to four ounces of weight. Of course, you don't actually get fifteen speeds, any more than you get ten speeds on a ten-speed bike, but you may get a touring bike that is able to leap tall buildings.

Shifting a fifteen-speed can be tricky, and an experienced cyclist is much more likely to profit from the close range of gears than a novice rider. Chainrings of 52/47/28 with a freewheel of 14/17/21/26/32 give thirteen distinct gears, including three very low ones. The low gear of 23.6 is low enough to ride up those rare 1:4 hills.

# Tandems

Doubles anyone? Someday I think I will liquidate my material possessions and buy a custom tandem, advertise for a captain, and go for a truly lengthy tour. I am a natural born stoker, preferring labor over management in any situation. I would work hard on a tandem never to let my partner down. Combining effort with another rider is very enjoyable. The unity is intense. Individuality is compromised, and it's a good lesson in acceptance and cooperation.

Nevertheless, such close quarters day after day, never catching up, never seeing a clear road ahead, and never breathing air that wasn't passed through first by a hard working cyclist would begin to wear like a burr in a sock. On a long trip, I would have to captain some or there would be mutiny below deck. I think I would have to walk alone at night to balance the fierce togetherness of day.

The greater mass of machine and riders increases momentum on the downslopes. Small hills are flattened in a slap, but the longer ones are tough. Overall, it's faster. Two tandem teams have crossed the continental United States in 10 days, 21 hours, and 45 minutes. That is an average of 220 to 340 miles per day, and it isn't all downhill from Santa Monica to New York.

Most tandems have special brakes (cantilever, disc, drum), extra strong wheels (40 or 48 spokes with 4- or 5-cross lacing), wide, tough tires, and 15 or 21 gears. Not cheap, a fully-equipped custom or semi-custom tandem will cost around $2,000. If you are interested in tandem touring, write the Tandem Club of America (see the References section at the back of this book).

# COMPONENTS Saddles

Saddles are the focus of a lot of attention, often negative. The slim shape is necessary in order to allow the thighs to move freely when pedaling. Designed to support a rider's weight on the bone structure, not the buttocks, a wider saddle would cause chafing. Racers use saddles that are narrower than tourists', but racers spend most of their time on the drops with their weight forward. Tourists ride more upright most of the time and sit further back on the saddle. Women usually need a wider saddle than men because of the greater distance between their pelvic bones.

Finding a comfortable saddle may be difficult, but start by eliminating the plastic saddle that comes on inexpensive ten-speeds. Not all plastic or molded nylon saddles are uncomfortable or even cheap. The best ones, often used for

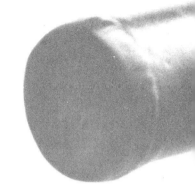

# Handlebars

racing because of their light weight, are covered with leather.

Leather saddles offer "give" plus support. Leather breathes, being porous, and wicks away sweat. It has to be broken in by a lot of riding but eventually will conform to the anatomy of the rider. A leather saddle should be saddle-soaped regularly and must be protected from the rain.

Recently, touring saddles have been designed for men and women by Avocet and Selle Milano. Wide across the back, the leather-covered plastic shell is cushioned under the contact points. The all leather Brooks B-72 is reputed to be comfortable for women. The shallow pubic arch in women forces the genitals against the nose of the saddle. Cutting a hole the appropriate size and location in the saddle would create a genuine woman's seat.

While flat bars can be used for touring, depending upon route and personal wishes, dropped bars are preferable for a number of reasons. They offer a greater variety of hand positions than do flat bars. The rider can lean forward a little or a lot. A better weight distribution results from using dropped bars, and steering and stability are improved. Arms absorb more shock, and a position in which the rider leans forward is easier on the spine than a straight upright posture. The gluteus maximus, the body's largest muscle, comes into play when the spine is lowered. Naturally, wind resistance is less.

Of the dropped bar designs, the Randonneur is best for touring. There is a slight bend that rises from the stem and gives a more upright position than other styles. Handlebars should allow a hold

# Brakes

that is at least shoulder wide so that breathing is not constricted.

Of course, one can lean over and use all the gluteus maximus one has when riding on flat bars. Millions of miles have been toured using flat bars, but I would tire much sooner if I rode them all day.

Padding on the bars lessens road shock to the fingers. Pressure from weight on the nerves in the palms may cause numbness, but the damage is only temporary. Riding on good United States and Canadian roads using correct technique on a bike adjusted to fit the rider, makes padding unnecessary.

The handlebar stem should not be raised out of the head tube past a line marked on the stem. Otherwise, it is possible to break the stem and damage the steering column—and the cyclist.

Center-pull brakes are standard on medium-priced bikes. They are slightly heavier and may not stop the bike quite as quickly as side-pull brakes, which are found on both low-priced and expensive bikes. Cantilever brakes, found on custom and tandem bikes, are the lightest and can be the most efficient. The brake levers should be positioned on the handlebars so that an easy reach is possible from both the top and the drops of the handlebars. Braking from the top is done when maximum braking is not needed. Rubber hoods on the levers increase comfort. I've also wrapped them with soft cloth.

Safety levers are really unsafe and should be removed. Using them contributes to instability when you need control. In order to actuate them, you must be in an upright position which places your weight too high.

Brake blocks consist of a metal holder and rubber pads or shoes. Pads are made with a great variety of surface designs and provide widely differing braking power. The larger the brake pad/rim contact area, the smaller the amount of heat buildup for a given unit of area. When they are hot, brake pads are less effective.

# Shifters

Bar-end, or fingertip shifters, are often preferred by tourists because it is not necessary to remove the hands from the handlebars to shift gears. This advantage is noticeable when pedaling uphill because it is then more difficult to keep balanced while shifting. Double shifting is easier with bar-end shifters. Shifters on the down tube are a little more trouble to get to, but they are more efficient. Being closer to the derailleurs, they use less cable and the cable path is straighter. Thus, they encounter less resistance in moving the derailleurs. Shifting is smoother. In order to better feel the shifting, you should move the levers with your hand, not just fingertips. Stem shifters have disadvantages and offer no advantages over the bar-end and down-tube shifters.

## Cranksets

## Pedals, Toe Clips, and Straps

An aluminum alloy, cotterless crankset is standard on good touring bikes. The swaged style, with crank and pins (or arms) in two pieces, is less expensive, yet still as reliable, as a forged, one-piece set, providing it has five pins, the rider is of average weight and he or she does not stomp on the pedals. I have a three-pin forged set which is certainly adequate for my weight and riding style. The better quality chainrings are forged and the alloy is hard. The inexpensive ones are stamped and soft, and wear out quickly from chain abrasion.

The minimum quality pedals for touring should have adjustable bearings and accommodate toe clips and straps. Toe clips are simple. They come in three sizes. Just make sure they are not too short or long. Pull the straps tight, particularly if pedaling in uncleated shoes.

*School holidays in Sweden.*

Nils-Johan Norenlind

# Trailers

I have a friend who works construction jobs and pulls his tools from job to job in his trailer. Because he is a fanatic, he loves it, but he will never say it's easy. Pulling a lot of weight in a trailer is easier, however, than carrying it on top of the bike. Light trailers weigh 20 to 25 pounds and cost about $200. Rolling and wind resistance are increased, but for some touring situations, they may be necessary. The first family that rode across the United States, the Wilhelms, pulled a trailer with all their gear. If the trailer fits, pull it.

Bill Woolston

# Racks
# and Packs

**Racks.** Stability is of primary importance. Carefully note the material, design, and method of attachment. For most purposes, a lightweight alloy is the best choice. In order to install a Blackburn front rack, I had to bend and file a groove in it to prevent the rack from interfering with my side-pull brakes. I've successfully used the inexpensive Pletscher rear rack (with seatstay support), with light loads but would not recommend it for long tours and heavy loads. Make sure the racks and bags are compatible.

**Seat bags.** The first place to put ad-

ditional weight on the bike is where it will be felt the least, that is, close to the rider's center of gravity, just behind the saddle. If small and compact, the seat bag is stable, but if large or insecurely attached, it will bounce and sway.

**Handlebar bags.** The most common place, and in some ways the least desirable place, to carry weight is between the handlebars. Convenience cannot be denied, but handling is compromised. Limit weight to ten pounds and make sure the bag is stable. Also, make sure the bag doesn't touch the front wheel and that there is clearance between the fingers and the bag.

**Panniers**. Panniers is a French word for bags and refers to the rack-mounted bags that hang down on both sides of the bike. To insure safety, look for stability in panniers as well as in racks. Examine construction for durability. Note the number of stitches, closures, and quality of material. Consider weather resistance. Canvas and nylon are both used. Cotton fibers swell when wet and provide some water resistance. Coated nylon is used more frequently because of its light weight. Seal the seams on the insides, if possible. Rain flaps are standard, but some are more effective than others. Pockets are convenient. A top flap which fastens with straps and buckles is a good design because carrying capacity is increased. A drawstring closure provides the best rain protection. The space is perfect for carrying food bought just before camping. Finally, consider visibility. Yellow or orange are the brightest colors.

# CLOTHING

Today I went cycling in all the wrong clothes and had a wonderful time. I planned to ride with my son to school a mile and a half away, then get a cup of coffee at my favorite cafe, run errands, and be at my desk by ten. Spring has been taking tentative nips at the Palouse lately, and today we got a soft, breezy nuzzle. I biked north, away from town, just to see where the road led. Much later an intersection allowed a turn west, then south, and an hour and a half later than planned, I got my coffee.

The roads were dirt more often than blacktop, and my three-speed steed loves a challenge. I had on Birkenstock sandals, patched wool socks, baggy yoga pants, flannel work shirt, and a floppy Japanese robe that doesn't button and isn't warm. Nobody could see by my outfit that I was a cyclist—an international rummage sale, perhaps. Actually, except for the robe which parachuted behind me and grabbed at the wind, the rest of the outfit had its merits. The shoes were stiff-soled, the socks and shirt warm, the baggy pants allowed movement.

Cruising around for just an hour or two, however, is different than touring for a month or more. I'm not willing to be so loose on tour. I want clothes that fit my needs as a cyclist, something between me and the hard knocks on the road, the chilling rain, the ever-hardening saddle.

With appropriate clothing you can cycle comfortably through a wide range in temperature. On tour, it may be sweltering in a valley, yet a few hours later may find you at the top of a snow-cloaked mountain pass. At first, special cycling clothes may look silly or their purpose may be inscrutable, but their special features gain meaning and value when their application is understood.

# Helmets

Wearing a hard-shell helmet is strongly recommended. Primarily, it protects the cyclist against the most frequent cause of cyclist death and permanent disability: brain injury. The level of protection a helmet offers is its most important feature; ventilation is next in importance.

Cycling builds up heat which escapes from the top of the head. Therefore, cycling helmets must be equipped with air vents. Being under a helmet when cycling slowly up a long, steep grade in hot weather feels a little like being in an oven. With a headband under the helmet, it's tolerable.

In cold conditions, the warmth a helmet provides is significant. Regardless of the temperature, I always wear a bandanna or visor under my helmet because I don't like the feel of the foam pads on my forehead. A headband also cushions the ride of the helmet. A cap or scarf under the helmet increases its warmth, especially on rapid descents in cool weather. Another way to keep cold air out is to block the air holes on the inside with tape or with foam plugs.

All helmets should have secure fastenings, be lightweight and not restrict vision or head movement. Removing your helmet and cycling with it attached to your panniers is like making love with the diaphragm in the dresser drawer. The freedom involves a risk.

Twice I've fallen and have resoundingly smacked my head. Both times the helmet has been there to take the blow. I cannot afford to lose any brain function. One of the knocks gave me a mild concussion anyway, which I found unusual as it served to quiet my neocortex and allowed the animal brain to speak. For three days, I was intuitive, wild-eyed, and in a high state of confusion.

# Mirrors

Rearview mirrors that attach to the helmet, to the wrist, or to the cyclist's glasses, enable the rider to know what is happening behind without his having to turn around to look. A mirror is not a substitute for turning and looking, which should always be done before maneuvers in traffic, but it can be used as an extra precautionary measure.

I appreciate my mirror, particularly when going downhill, because I can't hear traffic approaching behind me. Even though I may be going as fast, or nearly as fast, as a car and therefore take up a lane, I want to know what is at my back without having to turn around while traveling at high speed. Sooner or later, I expect to be passed by the vehicle behind me, and I like to know what it is. My ears, a mirror, and the cyclist's sixth sense provide me with rearview vision.

# Shirts
# and Shorts

Special shirts called cycling jerseys are made and, though a pleasure to own and wear, are not necessary for touring. The value of their features cannot be denied, but such features can be found in clothing that's probably already in your wardrobe. What's important is that the garment be close fitting yet unrestrictive, warm yet breathable, and long enough to cover the lower back when riding with the hands on the drops of the handlebars.

Cycling shorts, however, are unique. The best quality shorts are wool and have a chamois lining in the crotch. The chamois prevents abrasion better than any fabric and increases comfort, being a soft, second skin next to your own. The long cut prevents chafing on the inside of the thigh. The few and smooth seams, and the close fit, also help. The traditional black color hides dirt and the inevitable grease. If you wear shorts, particularly cut-off jeans with thick seams, you're asking for

double trouble.

Some people recommend wearing the chamois right next to the skin. While it might feel wonderful and be fine for my naturally drier, racing brothers, I prefer to wear 100 percent cotton underwear. Otherwise, the chamois would get especially damp and dirty in a very short time, and wool doesn't dry quickly enough to be washed out daily. Seamless, cotton briefs are the best bet for both men and women.

Use mild soap to wash cycling shorts or anything you wear next to your skin. Since chamois-lined wool shorts take a long time to dry, I rinse them out, soap or no soap, and strap them to the top of my rear panniers where they dry in the sun and wind. When the chamois hardens, treat it with oil.

Cycling shorts can be made at home to save money. If you sew your own, make sure to test ride them. Shorts of cotton and polyester with terry cloth lining are

## Gloves

also available. Not only are they inexpensive, they also dry quickly. Side pockets are a useful feature.

New or tight jeans are too restrictive to be good cycling wear. When dry, they're bulky and heavy; when wet, they're a ball and chain. If you want to take your jeans, do what John Rakowski does and wear old, loose ones. He gets 5000 miles of use before the seat wears through, and then either patches them or sells them to Rumanian teenagers.

Cycling gloves have padded leather palms, cloth mesh backs, and lack fingers. The padding helps prevent numb fingers from road shock and from the constant pressure of weight on the hands. Gloves also protect against abrasions resulting from a fall. While cycling gloves provide some buffer to the effects of cold, pressure, and scrapes, they will not alleviate discomfort that results from an improperly adjusted saddle or overlong stem.

# Shoes

Cycling shoes have many advantages over ordinary shoes. They have rigid soles which inhibit flex of the feet at the pedal and thereby allow the feet to transfer maximum force to the pedal. Cycling shoes are perforated, made of lightweight material, and are low-cut. These qualities contribute to an overall light weight. A cycling shoe should feel like part of your foot. Buy them tight because they stretch with wear. If you wear uncleated shoes, strap your feet in the toe clips as tightly as can be tolerated.

A few styles of running shoes are stiff enough and fit well enough to be usable, but if you plan to do something extraordinary with your feet for five to eight hours a day, why not use the footwear designed for that use?

Cleated shoes are more rigid and durable than the sneaker type. The purpose of the cleats, which are available in a variety of designs and materials, is to hold the foot firmly to the pedal so that no energy is lost in flex or sideways movement. With a stiff-soled and cleated shoe, the energy of the pedal stroke is concentrated at the ball of the foot. Cleats make pulling on the upstoke easier which contributes to the smoother cadence by distributing the effort among more muscles.

The traditional way of determining correct cleat placement is to ride in new shoes (without cleats) for fifty miles or until the marks on the shoe soles indicate where to position the cleats. Install cleats to aid in attaining the desirable parallel or the slightly toed-in position of the feet. Uncleated, rubber-soled cycling shoes may be used for walking, while shoes with cleats should be reserved only for cycling, tap-dancing, and Charlie Chaplin routines.

# Coldwear

An envelope of warm air keeps you warm. Your body heats the air near it, but the air needs to be held still and made to stay around. Something must impede the heated air as it rises and moves away. Fur, animal skin, leaves, newspaper, and plastic can all be donned for the sake of warmth. The most efficient way to insulate is to use layers of clothing. Exactly what should be worn as a first layer, right next to the skin, to provide the most warmth, is open to debate.

One view maintains that the first layer should be breathable, allowing the body's water vapor to pass through it. The layer next to the skin should rapidly wick water away to the outer layers of clothing and also insulate the body. Wool has been the traditional material used for insulation, although there are synthetic materials with fine wicking properties. The final protective layer is water-repellent, not waterproof. Gore-Tex is celebrated as a miracle fabric because it allows vapor to escape, but prevents rain from entering.

Others believe that an absolutely waterproof garment should be worn next to the skin as a vapor-barrier. The next and insulating layer will therefore remain dry and maximally effective. A waterproof, not water-repellent, jacket is then worn over the insulating layers.

Combining methods using vapor-barrier systems for the feet and sleeping bag, and a breathable system for the torso, legs, and arms, may provide the most comfort for cyclists.

**Upper body.** A good combination of layers for the torso and arms for cold weather cycling is a short-sleeved, wool undershirt or cycling jersey, then a close-knit, long-sleeved turtleneck, possibly an additional pullover or sweater, and, finally, a wind or rain protection layer.

**Hands.** Use liners or gloves inside mittens and a wind- or rain-proof outer mitten. Foam handlebar padding is much warmer to hold onto than a taped bar.

**Head.** Put a cap or scarf under your helmet and wrap a scarf around your neck. Tape or plug the air vents in the helmet. Some rain jacket hoods fit better over the helmet and others fit better under. Try your helmet on with the hood when buying a rain jacket. Make sure the hood doesn't interfere with vision to the side. If you don't use a helmet, wear a balaclava, or heavy, wool cap.

**Legs.** On the lower body, two layers are usually sufficient: an inner layer of cycling shorts, long johns or tights, and an outer layer of sweat pants, wool pants, tights, or knickers. Cycling tights are like long cycling shorts, with or without a chamois crotch, and are most commonly made of wool. The seat of sweat pants or tights can be reinforced for increased

strength in that high friction area. Rain pants over insulating layers provide additional protection against wind and wet. I usually wear a pair of baggy wool-blend pants on top of long underwear, but have occasionally worn three layers—long underwear, cycling shorts, and pants.

**Feet.** Wear thin socks under thicker ones. Silk liner socks are particularly warm and give protection against blisters. Shoes can be covered by waterproof booties or thick socks with holes cut to accommodate shoe cleats.

# Rainwear

If the rain is warm, relax and enjoy the bath. If the rain is cold but the day is hot, a shower can be refreshing. Usually, however, getting wet in the rain is a prelude to being cold.

A protective jacket or an anorak (which is a pullover style) should be long enough to cover the lower back when you are leaning over with your hands on the drops of the handlebars. The hood should not interfere with the field of vision and should have a drawstring closure. If you can't find such a hood, just wear a jacket and a separate rain hat. The jacket can be pulled close to the body to reduce wind resistance, if the waist has a drawstring. Neck and wrist openings should close snugly, too, yet the rain gear should not constrict movement, even when layers of clothing are worn underneath. Zippers should be covered in order to keep rain out and to eliminate cold spots. The fabric should be moderately abrasion-resistant and brightly colored for visibility.

The best buy is a jacket that is useful in all seasons. In winter, it can be worn on top of several layers, and in summer it can be worn on top of a light shirt. The most suitable rain pants for cycling have elastic bands and zippers, or Velcro closures, around the ankles to prevent mix-ups with the chainring. Some cyclists prefer using a rain cape. A cape allows air to circulate and permits less chance of getting soaked with sweat.

# Hotwear

Cotton's faults in cold weather become virtues in hot weather. Highly absorbent, a long-sleeved cotton shirt or pullover, damp with sweat, cools you as you ride. When water is plentiful, soak your shirt and douse your head and hair. Loose clothes increase the cooling effect, and light-colored garments reflect heat. The head, neck, backs of hands, and calves should be covered from the sun above and from reflection all around. Being cooled by moving, you may not realize that your skin is cooking. It's foolish to ride shirtless, not only because of sunburn, but because a fall without a shirt or jacket could result in a major laceration instead of a minor abrasion. Thin socks aid evaporation from the feet. Silk socks next to the feet help prevent blisters.

Be very careful. Cover up from head to toe, protect your skin with sunscreens, soothe it with creams or aloe vera, and protect your eyes with a sun visor and dark glasses.

# Clothing List

The following items are suggested for a summer tour to include a variety of weather conditions:

- Cycling shoes
- Cycling shorts
- Regular shorts which can be used as a bathing suit
- A cotton long-sleeved shirt, such as long underwear
- A wool or pile, long-sleeved shirt, such as a turtleneck pullover
- One or two cotton short-sleeved shirts
- A wool short-sleeved shirt, such as a cycling jersey
- Sweater, wind shirt, or jacket
- Two pairs of pants, one of loose cotton and one of wool
- A pair of cycling tights, long johns, sweat pants, or warm-up pants
- Two pairs of cotton underpants
- Rain protection, including jacket or cape, perhaps gaiters, rain pants, or shoe covers
- Gloves, either cycling gloves or ordinary gloves, and perhaps mittens or overmitts
- Two or three pairs of socks, one thin pair such as silk liner socks and one wool pair
- Two bandannas, used as headband, nose wiper, pot-holder, water filter, dust mask, napkin, bandage, neck protector, pouch, dishrag, washrag, or grease rag
- Sunglasses

I've always taken less than ideal weather protection. I've had no trouble staying cool, but I couldn't count on being warm, and occasionally, the only thing still dry at the end of the day was my sense of humor. For my first tour I borrowed a tent which kept out mosquitoes but not the rain. Rain gear consisted of a plastic poncho which kept me wet with sweat. My jacket was a cherished one, old and velvet—not in the least water-repellent. I counted on "riding out of the rain" as the surest way to stay warm. Cafes were my most frequent rain protection. In addition to being waterproof, they're breathable and friendly.

By my second tour, I had bought a waterproof tent and I relished the increased independence and comfort. I found a Chinese silk jacket at a rummage sale—no hood, zippers, drawstrings or wrist closures. Nevertheless, it was the warmest jacket I've ever owned as long as I wrapped a scarf around my neck to block the wind. "Was" because I lost it on the last day of my trip. Still using my old plastic poncho as a jacket, I remained wet when it rained. I now own an expensive jacket that's waterproof. It provides a lot of warmth by trapping body heat. Now I'm only damp with sweat, which is an improvement. The plastic poncho has been demoted to bike-cover and ground cloth, functions for which it is perfectly suited.

# Materials

Cotton

Ventile

Cotton/nylon

Cotton/polyester

Wool

Wool Blends

Nylon

Uncoated Nylon

Coated Nylon

Ripstop Nylon

Nylon Taffeta

Oxford

Cordura

Pile

Cotton is warm when dry, cool when wet. Highly absorbent. When wet, cotton takes a long time to dry and does not provide insulation.

Ventile is 100 percent cotton. Tightly woven, strong, heavy, and water-repellent. When damp, the threads swell, closing the gaps, making the fabric more water-resistant while retaining its breathability.

Cotton/nylon or 60/40 cloth and cotton/polyester are generally more durable and lighter than 100 percent cotton but are less warm. They are wind-resistant and breathe easily.

Wool usually is less comfortable than cotton next to the skin but remains warm when wet. Body heat will dry out wool next to the skin. Wool fiber absorbs up to 30 percent of its weight before it begins to "feel" wet. If thoroughly wet, it takes a long time to dry out.

Wool blends are less expensive, more abrasion-resistant, often lighter, but slightly less warm than 100 percent wool. Avoid blends of less than 65 percent wool. Wool's characteristics make it appropriate for summer and winter use.

Nylon is stronger, often lighter than cotton, and is abrasion-resistant. A material of 1.9-ounce nylon is heavier and generally sturdier than one of 1.6-ounce nylon.

Uncoated nylon is wind-resistant, fully breathable, but not water-repellent.

Coated fabrics have increased water-repellency, but condensation occurs on the inside of the garment.

Ripstop nylon, coated and uncoated, contains a grid of reinforcing threads which increases tear strength.

Nylon taffeta is dense, strong, windproof, and slightly water-repellent. Oxford and cordura are types of nylon taffeta.

Cordura is coarsely woven, strong, heavy, water-repellent and highly abrasion-resistant. Waterproof coatings don't take to cordura as well as they do other nylons.

Pile is a nylon material that is as warm as wool but lighter. Body heat will dry it completely, and it is warm when wet. Wind blows through, however, and it is bulky and scratchy.

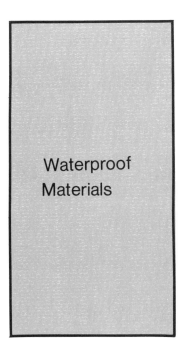

Waterproof
Materials

Plastic

Plastic is inexpensive and water-proof, allowing neither rain in nor sweat out. Good for ground-cloths, bike covers, and bike bag linings but not for raincoats.

Neoprene

Neoprene, or rubber cloth, is strong but heavy.

Vinyl

Vinyl, a plastic used on cotton, is strong and heavy.

Urethane or Polymer

Urethane or polymer is used on nylon. The more used, the greater the water-resistance and weight.

Gore-Tex

Gore-Tex is lightweight, breathable, and waterproof. It consists of a film of polytetrafluorethylene with a nylon fabric bonded to one or both sides. The film contains nine billion pores per square inch. The pores are too small for water drops to enter, but large enough to allow water vapor to escape. Body heat pushes the vapor through the fabric. Expensive.

# Fillers

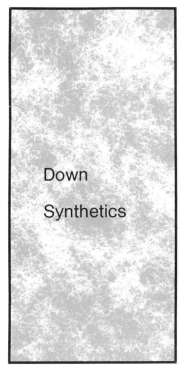

Down
Synthetics

Down

Down is the most effective insulation per pound. Best for cold, dry conditions. Worthless when wet. Light, compressible, and resilient, it retains loft for many years of use. Down's ability to loft is measured in cubic inches per ounce of down. Down presently ranges from 350 to 700 cubic inches per ounce. High and low grades are generally mixed in down products. "Prime" is a subjective term. Look for the highest loft-per-pound or cubic-inch-per ounce ratio when buying.

Synthetics

Synthetics provide insulation and warmth when saturated. Polyester absorbs less than one percent of its weight in moisture and retains loft. It compresses less than down, which means it takes up more room in packing. Wet or dry, it provides more insulation under the sleeper. Synthetics are heavier than down, but cheaper.

Thinsulate

Thinsulate is a synthetic which has less bulk than other synthetics, but provides equal insulation.

# TECHNIQUE

Riding an adult bicycle packed with camping equipment day after day on unfamiliar roads is not the same as the pedaling we did as kids on clunkers around the neighborhood. As the first machine mass-produced for personal transportation, the bicycle has always been loved for the freedom it brings. I bought my children their first bikes when they were 6 and 8. On their delighted faces, I saw (and remembered) the realization that the world had suddenly opened. They were gone in a flash, experiencing their new release from home. In my grown-up heart, I knew that they would soon return shocked, in tears, having discovered that the seductive freedom also brings blood and bruises.

With age comes maturity and, with a little bit of luck, attendant wisdom. Adult cyclists hope to tour with a minimum amount of pain. The expectation is that you will return home in better shape than you have been in for years. You will meet a variety of geographic features, weather conditions, and road surfaces. It will not always be pleasant, but it will certainly be memorable. All of the challenges, thrills—and jeopardy—of cycling up and down hills, bouncing on dirt, and riding in windy, rainy, hot, and dry weather are there.

Good touring technique will insure that you do have a comfortable tour and return home in good shape, and in one piece. As with all sports, there are certain basic practices that result in efficiency and safety.

"The resurgence of cycling has put a generation on the road without knowledge of either the craft or the sport of cycling," states John Forester, the former president of the League of American Wheelmen. Cycling clubs can offer this knowledge through observation, discussion, and direct experience. Reading about technique is also valuable, but a bit like painting a house. At first, it looks worse. However, augmented by riding, reading will instill confidence. Riding is more important, though. Read, then go ride a bike.

# Hand Positions

There are three basic correct hand positions for use with the turned-down style handlebars most common to ten-speed bikes. The first is with the hands placed on the top of the handlebars, near the stem, wrists straight, knuckles forward. A variation of this is to move the hands away from the stem a few inches. This position allows the most upright body position and will feel the most comfortable over a long period of time.

When riding on the "tops," head movement is very free, thus vision from side to side is unhampered.

The second position is with hands on top of the handlebars, near the brake levers, wrists straight, thumbs forward. A variation is to place the crotch of the thumb on top of the brake hoods. This position offers good control of the bike and easy braking. The body position is somewhat lowered, which slightly increases pressure on the hands and strain on the back.

The third position is with hands on the "drops," wrists straight. Wind resistance is the least in this position, and power output is maximized. Braking is easy and powerful. This position is used for fast riding and for slogging through strong headwinds. Two variations of this position are often seen and are incorrect. In the first, the fingers grasp the bar right beneath the brake levers. In the second, hands are at the very end of the handlebars.

In Tai Chi, it is said one will break the chi by bending the wrist, and students are asked to allow an unobstructed passage for the chi, clear to the ends of the fingers. A joint of the body is strengthened, just like one in a bicycle frame, by creating a connection. Nearly-straight wrists make more effective connections than do bent ones. If you feel you have to stretch to reach the brakes, adjust the position of your saddle or handlebars.

Equally important is to hold the

*Hands on the drops.*

*The RV of the past and the RV of the future.*

handlebars without undue tension. Energy spent choking the handlebars is wasted. Fingers gripping the bars like a baseball bat will not be sensitive to the road surface. One rides a bike, not throttles it.

If it is necessary to ride one-handed, keep the hand that is on the bike near the center of the bars for stability. I also feel fairly secure holding onto the brake hoods.

Elbows should be slightly bent, not locked straight. A stiff, rigid connection breaks easily and is soon not a connection. It is ideal to be loose, relaxed, aware, and ready to receive—never locked, tight, and ready to shatter. Bent elbows act as shock absorbers. If you want to go faster, increase the bend at your elbows. As you lean over, wind resistance is reduced and powerful muscles come into play. If you feel you have to press the weight of your upper body on the handlebars in order to stay on the saddle, or if you have neck and back pain, the seat needs to be adjusted, perhaps tilted back slightly.

# Pedaling

Power goes from the rider's feet to the pedals, to the chainring, to the chain, to the freewheel, to the right spokes, to the left spokes, and you move. Most cyclists apply pressure to the pedals for only three hours out of the possible twelve of the circle, from about two o'clock to five o'clock. Obviously, if cyclists spent more of the clockface working, output would increase. What cyclists should do is pedal around the circle, not just push on the down-stroke. Different muscles are used for different parts of the stroke. To instill the habit of "round pedaling," pull with the thigh while relaxing the calf.

The main purpose of toe clips, cleats, and straps is to position the foot properly on the pedal and to join the bike and the rider. Proper foot position is extremely important. The spindle of the pedal should lie directly under the ball of the foot. This allows maximum leverage. The foot and

74

# Cadence

the pedal should act as one unit. Feet may be toed-in slightly when pedaling, knees should come close to the top tube. However, rickshaw drivers pedal huge loads all day in sandals in a fixed gear and have never heard of round pedaling.

"The most efficient pedal stroke utilizes the *natural motion* of the foot," say Mike Kolin and Denise de la Rosa, cycling coaches and writers. As the foot is lifted, in walking or pedaling, the heel is higher than the toes. As the foot descends, the heel and toes become level and then the heel begins to lead the toes toward the ground to complete the stroke. At a high pedaling rate, the toe is below the heel at the bottom of the stroke, but not because the rider consciously directs it there. If I think about my feet at all, I concentrate on the position of my heels. I follow them around with my mind's eye. As long as my foot isn't fixed and wooden like a mannequin's or pointed like a ballerina's, I'm satisfied.

Cadence is the rate of pedaling measured in revolutions per minute. It can be either high or low. "Spinning," which implies a high rpm, is the look of healthy cadence and of thriving pedal action. A rider who believes that because everything hurts, he must be doing it right, is wrong. A high rpm is recommended because muscles can be conditioned to perform a large number of light repetitions in a shorter time than it takes to train muscles to double the amount of force they can exert.

In one study, seven road racers rode their own racing bikes on a treadmill moving 20 mph and inclined to a 3.5 percent grade. Each rider selected the cadence most comfortable for him. Their choices averaged out to 91 rpm. When tested at a rate 20 rpm slower and 20 rpm faster than their ideal rates, they were less efficient, as shown by an increase in oxygen consumption and lactic acid production.

# Steering

All cyclists are encouraged to spin because it is more efficient. To determine your cadence, count your pedal revolutions for six seconds and multiply by ten to get the rate per minute. If it isn't 60, use a lower gear and increase your rate until 60 is reached. Practice until it feels natural. Then head for 70. At 80 you get a gold star and the satisfaction that you're right up there with the best of the tourists.

On the road, cadence is in a state of flux. It should be maintained by shifting. For example, accelerate from a stand-still to 70 rpm in a low gear, shift and the rpms will drop to fifty, then accelerate up to 70 rpm again, shift and on it goes. In general, a heavy person will have a lower cadence than a light person. Wearing cycling shoes with cleats will help you to achieve a good cadence.

The primary skill to develop is riding in a straight line at a nearly constant cadence. Then learn how to maintain a straight line while turning around to check traffic behind you. A safe way to do this is to raise off the saddle a bit, turn slightly at the hips and then look back. Looking behind you should always be done before changing lanes and any other maneuvers in traffic.

Steering seems almost to happen by itself. You lean ever so slightly, and a turn happens. A good bike is stable and steers itself, wanting to remain upright. It tries to stay under your weight. A sensitive bike is quick to follow lean—yours or the road's. Sensitive steering is a disadvantage on very rough roads, but a front rack and panniers will dampen the bike's tendency to shimmy.

There are times when it is necessary to turn quickly, such as to miss a rock or hole. A quick turn must be forced without the usual anticipatory and unconscious lean. If a car pulls right out in front of you, you'll have to turn instantly. Force a quick, sharp turn in the opposite way from which you need to go to avoid the car. This jerk in the wrong direction forces a lean in the direction you want to go. Then turn back sharply so the bike can get under you again. These emergency turns seem instinctive to me, but it's a good idea to practice them in a parking lot and analyze what transpires. Basically, there is a radical split between bike and rider and a quick reunification.

# Shifting

The derailleur can shift only when the chain is moving and has slight, even tension on it. To shift, reduce the pressure being applied to the pedals, keep pedaling, shift, continue pedaling until the chain drops into position and catches on the teeth of the sprocket. If pedaling uphill and a shift is necessary, get your speed up a bit, reduce pressure on pedals but keep pedaling, then shift. The chain is seated properly when it runs silently through the derailleurs and around the rear sprocket. If you hear the chain rubbing after changing gears, adjust the shifters to position the derailleurs properly.

Attempt to maintain a fairly constant rate of pedaling by shifting gears. Know

*Feathering on the downhill.*

where your chain is and think ahead about how to shift in order to accommodate changes in terrain or conditions. Shift down before a steep ascent. If the hill is low or short, you can stand up and power over it in a higher gear than you would need if you remained seated. You can also lean over and press hard for just a few minutes. Power is increased in both positions. Around town, I change my body positions according to the terrain. While on tour, however, I stay seated and use the bike's resources to go over hills. At the beginning of the day or after a long rest or downhill coast, use low gears and spin to warm up cold muscles. Remember to gear down just before stopping.

A wind is like a hill. Shift to accommodate it. Three of the four directions the wind blows from are a hindrance to the cyclist. Watch for open places where a blast might catch you off guard. A wind from the fourth direction, a tailwind, offers the rare opportunity to sit up straight, fluff your feathers out, shift into high gear, and pedal fast, all at once.

In traffic, ride in low to medium gear so that you are ready to accelerate quickly as the traffic flow demands. Don't get stuck in high gear at a red light.

# Braking

Keep in mind that brakes only stop the wheels. All the weight on the bike wants to continue forward. Naturally, a loaded bike takes longer to stop under the best of conditions and most careful application of brakes. If the brakes are applied too hard or too quickly, it's possible that you and the bike can flip over the front wheel. Apply the rear brake first, then the front and apply firm, even pressure. If the rear wheel begins to skid, too much weight is forward. Ease up. If you must stop quickly, apply more force to the front brake than to the rear, but not to the point

of forcing a skid in the rear. Push yourself back and down in order to resist the forward weight transfer.

When going downhill, control speed by "feathering" your brakes. Squeeze them gently, then let go. Feathering prevents the rims and pads from overheating. Don't turn and brake at the same time. Brake first, then enter the turn.

Braking is slowed by wet rims. Steel rims are the worst, but even with alloy rims stopping usually takes at least twice, often three times as long as stopping under dry conditions. After going through

puddles, squeeze the brakes lightly to wipe off the water on the rims. For the most responsive braking, have the brake system adjusted so that there is minimum cable friction and minimum clearance between the brake blocks and rims.

Braking can be done from the top or from the drops of the handlebars. From the drops, fingers wrap around the brake lever and pull back. From the tops, with hands on the brake hoods, fingers push more down than back. The top position is not as powerful, but is sufficient for normal speed control.

# Up

When climbing, attempt to keep rpms as high as possible for as long as possible. Shift gears and gradually increase leg effort. When that becomes impossible—you're down to the lowest gear and can't keep a fast cadence—try to relax. Settle down to the long haul ahead with a pedaling rate you know you can maintain for hours. Concentrate on pedaling smoothly. Set short, temporary goals such as the next curve, the tall pine ahead. Look around and enjoy the scenery.

Standing up and pedaling allows use of different muscles. It gives variety in a tedious climb and feels like an additional low gear. Holding on around the brake-lever hoods provides a stable position for riding out of the saddle.

Stay seated most of the time, if possible, and vary hand position on the tops where breathing is easier. Occasionally, lean down and use the drops. More power is available in that position because the gluteus maximus joins the effort. The back tires in this position relatively quickly. I like to tie my jacket around my waist. The increased heat to my lower back feels good. I also sit on the jacket, adding a little comfort to a stressful grind. If you stop for a rest, make it a quick one. Keep the direction of your energy going uphill. Don't scatter your concentration. Legs get cold quickly, and, after a rest, pedaling uphill is painful until everything gets flowing again.

Because speed is slow going uphill, stay to the right and let cars pass. If the right side of the road is dangerous, stay to the inside, left of the shoulder line. Ride in a straight line so that cars behind know what to expect. When the road is deserted, many cyclists will switch back and forth across both traffic lanes which considerably lessens the incline. The practice is not safe, but is very common. On inside curves (to the right), avoid the steep inside bank by crossing to the outside of the lane. On outside curves, stay to the outside because it is an easy coast down to the other lane, but it is a steep climb back out again. At the top of the grade, walk around, eat, drink, check your tires, brakes, racks, and packs. Make sure the brake quick-releases haven't somehow opened. Put on a jacket and/or a dry T-shirt for the breezy, chilly descent.

# Down

To descend at a speed on the slower side of possibility, sit up and use your body as a brake. With hands on the brake hoods, apply the brakes lightly. "Feather" them to control your speed. To descend, lean over, hands on the drops, elbows bent, feet horizontal, thighs bracing the saddle, and weight back and on the pedals. Knees and elbows should be spring-like, able to absorb bumps. Or, you can lean over and have your weight on the saddle to rest your legs.

In any case, always be ready to brake. Weight should be rearward, and consciousness should be forward. Observe the road ahead very carefully for rocks, bumps, holes, carcasses, gravel, intersections, glass, oil, parked cars, sharp curves, and broken bridges. Beware of crosswinds lying in wait around curves. On long descents, use both brakes equally to prevent one rim from overheating. I always use my body as a braking force first, then the brakes. I have, however, worn out brake blocks from mile after mile of nearly continuous braking going down a long pass in a rainstorm.

During a rapid descent is the time for heightened awareness and extra caution. If you fall going uphill, the greatest injury may be to your pride. But if you fall going downhill, you are likely to bring your bicycle camping tour to a disappointing, expensive, and painful end. The thought of leaving bits of my lovely flesh attached to the asphalt is enough to keep me very, very alert. I do not look at the scenery. I do not think about my stomach or love life. Those are uphill entertainments.

In spite of, and because of, the danger, downhills will always be very popular with cyclists. They provide time for rest and time for exhilaration. My favorite descent took place unexpectedly on one of the countless hills in the Oregon coastal range. We had turned off frenetic Highway 101 onto a road blocked to auto traffic by barricades and signs that warned "Bridge Out." Obediently deserted, the road led uphill. The bridge was out, but we simply belayed our bikes and gear down into the gulley and up the other side. In a flash, we were off. Knowing to a great degree of certainty that no cars would be coming up, we had the unusual freedom to corner, coast, and pedal for miles downhill with only ourselves to think about.

Unless the downhill is straight, I avoid the most aerodynamic tuck position. Usually, a downhill section is full of corners. The safest way to negotiate a corner is to brake before entering the curve and coast through it in as straight a line as possible within your own traffic lane. If you want to go fast, lower your center of gravity by putting your weight on the pedals. Putting your weight on *one* pedal lowers the center of gravity even further. To coast around a corner at a high speed, lean in the direction of the turn until your nose is approximately over your hand. The inside pedal must, repeat must, be raised and the outside pedal must be down. Concentrate your weight on the outside, or downhill, leg.

To pedal around a corner, keep the bike upright. Move your upper body in the direction of the curve until your nose is over your hand, but don't tilt the bike so much that the inside pedal will scrape the ground at the bottom of the pedal stroke.

Coast over bumps, weight on the pedals with elbows and knees loose. Think light. Don't be a deadweight and bounce on the saddle like a dude. Let the bike move under you. Give it rein.

When descending rapidly, the wind in your ears will drown out the noise of approaching traffic. At these times, I most appreciate having a rearview mirror. Quick glances keep me informed and prepared for a passing car. When your speed is nearly that of the traffic, take up a lane and stay away from the shoulder or edge of the road.

Make the cars stay behind you until it's safe for them to pass. Use hand signals to indicate "Stay where you are" or "OK to pass." I move over a bit and may brake slightly or sit up to slow my speed in order to give the driver time to get around me before the next curve.

Usually, cars will give you plenty of room behind and when passing. A good driver behind you can provide relief, even protection on a descent. I acknowledge courtesy and intelligence with a nod or smile when I'm passed.

Occasionally, the front wheel will begin to wobble on a rapid descent. It may be caused by many factors: the pitch of the road bumps coinciding with their frequency, untrue wheels, out-of-round wheels, loose spokes, loose hub, loose headset, uneven weight distribution, too high a center of gravity, or bent forks. To control wobble, grip the bars firmly, use the rear brake more than the front, and slow down as quickly as possible.

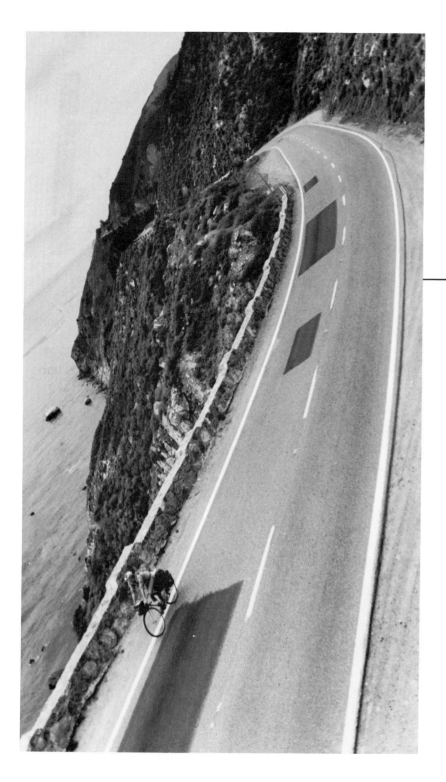

# Drafting

If one rider follows closely behind another who is moving fairly fast, the follower enjoys reduced air resistance. This means the follower can go as fast as the first but with less effort. A distance of a foot or less is the most effective distance, but also the most dangerous. Where, exactly, to position oneself when drafting depends upon the road and the wind, if it is blowing. Sometimes, a position directly behind the leader is most effective, sometimes slightly to the right or the left. Do not overlap the wheel of the rider ahead. If the wheels touch, the second rider may be flipped and hit by other cyclists.

The drafting rider develops split vision, with one eye on the wheel of the cyclist ahead and the other on the road ahead. The lead cyclist has the responsibility of watching the road well ahead, steering safely and gently away from hazards, and maintaining a constant pace. The lead cyclist should indicate rocks, glass, or other dangers and should clearly signal turns.

Drafting enables an overall higher average speed and can be used to great advantage. One disadvantage for touring is that it takes intense concentration, particularly when learning. The energy might be more enjoyably spent on appreciating the scenery. I'm not skilled enough to draft and relax at the same time. I resort to a close draft only in strong head winds or when trying to make a destination before dark.

In a group, the weaker riders can be pulled along by the stronger ones who rotate the lead position. This evens out the overall ability of the group. In a strong headwind, drafting is the only way to ride. Since cycling in wind is not most people's idea of fun, drafting enables the party to get to a windless day faster.

Certain phrases and actions are standard communication between cyclists riding together. "On your wheel," or something similar, should be said when you come up behind another to draft. Also, let the rider ahead know when you decide to fall back or pass. "On your left," indicates you are passing. "Car back," is a warning that a car is approaching from the rear. Cyclists riding two abreast may merge into a single file line.

# Pace

Pace is as individual as you are. I like Woody Allen's pace, namely, lying in bed with a friend, eating Chinese takeout, and watching old movies on TV. Strive for a balance between your energy output and your body's ability to synthesize energy. There is a pace that works best for you, and that will change from time to time. Conditioning, not size, determines the pace you ride. The goal is to last from dawn to dusk. Pace, don't punish.

Part and parcel of group touring is the slowest rider. Nobody wants to be "it," but maligned or appreciated, the slow rider is here to stay. The overall pace should be determined by what that person can do. It is not necessary, or even desirable, that everyone ride in a clump like a tank division. Contact between the group members can be maintained, even if sporadic lapses occur, when a fast rider spurts ahead for several miles. The fast riders can circle back and ride the miles again with the slower ones. The fast riders can drink more beer, which, eventually, will cause greater equality among the group members. In any case, at least one other person should ride with or near the slow one. It is demoralizing to feel that the best you can do isn't socially acceptable. The slow rider—the old one, or the child, or the one with the heavy bike—should take a turn at leading the pack like anyone else. It's very important that each member get a chance to see the road ahead unobstructed by a cyclist's rear, attractive though it may be.

Bikes have a pace too. A fourteen-pounder feels like a just-broken colt, whereas a thirty-pounder is matronly and sedate.

# ON THE ROAD

Finding the "optimum route through the quagmire" is the joy of Laurence Malone, national cyclo-cross champion. "The one less traveled by" is the path that makes all the difference, whatever that may be, says poet Robert Frost. The bicycle camper counsels, "Seek the secondary and tertiary networks." All suggest that there might be a better way than the beaten path.

Choosing the less traveled path can be planned ahead. Study maps and aim for the tiny line that wanders away from the wider, darker one. Or, turn to the lesser-known byway impulsively.

Last summer on the North Cascade Highway near Winthrop, Washington, a motorcyclist pulled up beside me and gestured to pull over. I assessed all the cues and concluded he was no risk. Besides, the road was busy with vacationers.

"Wanna avoid a lot of hills?" he asked, grinning, thumbs hooked in his belt under his belly, hefty legs holding his Harley steady on the incline.

"Depends upon whether they're up or down," I answered. I wanted time to plumb his meaning, but I smiled, figuring he was going to offer a tow.

"Both," he returned squarely, not taking up my joke. "When you get to the bridge turn left across the river. Ignore all the signs. They're for the tourists. Takes 'em over a lot of extra hills and through another town so they can all stop and get a postcard or some junk to take home."

I thanked him politely, but kept my enthusiasm in check. From the maps I had seen, I was on the one and only road that led over the two North Cascade passes. This guy is probably kidding, I thought.

Has his fun misdirecting tourists.

A few miles further, to my half-surprise, a real enough intersection appeared. The left turn crossed a bridge, while the right, well-marked North Cascade Highway, paraded uphill. If I turn left, I thought, I'll probably end up back in Spokane. Perhaps it leads to his driveway and he's a rich pervert and this is a trap. Everyone else was turning right.

Hmmm. Why not? I turned left. And the road was lovely and level, following a river. Pastures grew and old houses withdrew alongside the quiet road. Occasionally I caught sight of the incredibly juvenile Cascade Highway, hopping and skipping around the hills across the valley. Soon my road and the big one met. I was at no loss in altitude and I began seriously to climb toward the passes.

America is a rich land, rich in its people. I've received many blessings on my tours, gifts of food and shelter, lifts through snow and gravel, homemade talk from just plain folks, and dreams and revelations from the Source. A trip deserves my best efforts. I want to go not expecting gifts, but knowing they may be offered. Being human and given any excuse to think highly of ourselves, we usually will. Riding on fewer wheels than normal and using our body-based fuels is a tempting excuse. Try to pack in a little humility with the semi-permeable rain gear and titanium bolts. A group of bicyclists converging upon a cafe is still a group of bikers and not necessarily any less disruptive than the leather-jacketed kind. Unless you're sure you've got special dispensation from God, don't forget your money or your ID.

# Heat

Whether the humidity is high or low, respect hot weather and take precautions when cycling in it. First of all, carry plenty of water. Plenty means enough to last between each safe water supply. Avoid drinking water from a stream or ditch. Use water you find to douse your head and soak your clothes. For once, the wind chill factor will work in your favor. However, the cooling effect of rapid evaporation can mislead you into believing you're cooler than you really are.

Heat and empty spaces are often associated. Make sure when you start across an isolated stretch of country that you know how far ahead food and water are. Don't count on desert towns being inhabited. Mapmakers get nervous when they have an area on the map with a lot of empty space. They note the presence of old water holes, prospectors' graves, anything. Ask your Last Chance exactly what's ahead and how far it is. The front panniers could be used exclusively for water when cycling through hot, isolated stretches.

Muscles don't work as effectively in heat. The heart has to pump harder as blood vessels near the skin and in muscles dilate to increase blood flow and heat transfer. Set mileage goals that take into account lowered performance.

Cover up and protect your skin with long-sleeved, long-legged, white, loose, cotton clothes. Wear gloves, a scarf, sun-shade and dark glasses. Use lip balm or a sun screen. Avoid salt pills. Salt is better replaced by eating watermelon, celery, or kelp. Avoid drinks such as coffee, cola, and alcohol because they're diuretic. Ice cold and heavily sugared drinks should be avoided because they're somewhat shocking. Strong sugar solutions draw water away from other parts of the body to the intestines and contribute to dehydration. Even orange juice is too concentrated. Dilute sugar drinks with water.

Bonnie Wong

Bonnie Wong

Drink lots and lots of water. Drink whether you feel thirsty or not. Eat fruit, especially melons. Avoid heavy meals. Don't get anywhere near heatstroke. Then at the end of a hot, dry day, enjoy the incomparable pleasure of a cold beer or two.

Heatstroke is very serious and requires immediate attention. The core temperature of the body rises too much. Water intake does not compensate for fluid lost by sweating. Heat exhaustion occurs before heatstroke. If you suspect that you or someone in your group is approaching heat exhaustion, get out of the heat as quickly as possible. The victim's skin will be flushed and feel hot and dry. He will experience a rapid pulse, throbbing head, irregular vision and disturbed thinking. Unconsciousness can result. The affected person should sip liquids, if possible, and be sponged with water, particularly about the head and face.

In the hottest part of the day, take a siesta. If there isn't shade, make some. Tie a ground cloth to a fence, bush or bike. Riding in intense heat can be completely avoided by cycling before dawn and quitting when the day gets hot. Spend the rest of the afternoon in a city swimming pool, public library, air-conditioned theater, or friendly tavern. In the evening, three or four more hours are available for cycling. This method of crossing hot places requires nicely-spaced towns and an easy-going attitude.

# Wind

The prevailing wind direction across an area can make a difference in selecting a route. Most people ride across the United States from west to east because of the prevailing summer winds. If I were to make a loop to the ocean and back from where I live in northern Idaho, I would return east along the Columbia River gorge, taking advantage of the strong tail wind that blows through the gorge from the west. Usually wind doesn't do the cyclist any favors.

In addition to Mother Nature's wind, there's the inevitable drag created by the cyclist and bike moving through the air. Wind resistance increases as speed increases. A tail wind will demonstrate the power of wind resistance by eliminating it. Suddenly, you realize that you're cruising effortlessly in high gear, though the road is level. There's no whistle in your ears and you don't feel a thing on your face. The grass on the side of the road leans in the direction you're going. It takes nine times as much effort to pedal a bike at 12 mph into a 6-mph wind as it does to pedal the same bike at the same speed with the wind

*Head winds mean work.*

from behind. A tail wind on tour is a pleasure equal to that of home-style hashbrowns—and as rare.

When a big truck roars past in the opposite lane and there is also a side wind from that direction, the wind blast following the truck is particularly strong. Fast and constant traffic will create a draft that will push you along as a tail wind would. Of course, a tail wind without traffic is preferable, but the draft is one small compensation for traffic.

The windchill factor inherent in cycling bears heavily upon the safety and comfort of the rider. In the heat, it's a relief, but in the wet or cold, it can be dangerous. On a cold day of 40 degrees Fahrenheit, a wind at 20 mph (or a cycling speed of 20 mph), means the effective temperature, or cooling power of the wind, is 18 degrees Fahrenheit. When wet, the chill is increased dramatically as the thermal conductivity of water is 240 times greater than that of still air.

# Rain

Slower cycling and greater caution are always required when riding in the rain because of the chilling factor of wind and water and the increased danger of falling. Beware of oily spots, wet leaves, painted lines, and metal such as manhole covers, tracks, and bridge surfaces. As the rain mixes with the oil on the road, the surface becomes slippery. After the road is washed, it's less slippery, but hydroplaning can result during heavy downpours. The tires skim the surface and float on the water rather than maintain tension with the road surface. Go slowly through puddles and wipe off the rims by gentle, periodic braking. If you begin to skid, push your weight back, pump the brakes, and steer into the skid to keep the bike upright.

The combinations of wind and rain, or even wind and sweat, can cause the body temperature to drop very quickly. If the body loses heat faster than it produces it, hypothermia can result. Anytime wind and wet are combined, beware of this condition. Hypothermia can occur in mild temperatures of 30 to 50 degrees Fahrenheit. I'm always delighted to see a long, steady uphill grade when it's raining. I know I'm not going to stay dry, but at least my body will generate heat.

If you are planning to tour in wet weather, use fenders and alloy rims. Wear bright yellow and lights, such as the blinking Belt Beacon. Make sure the brakes are well adjusted. Brake pads that are longer than the usual two inches improve wet braking performance. Contrary to common belief, slotted and grooved pad surfaces do not give better wet braking performance, at least according to tests conducted at the Massachusetts Institute of Technology. If the rain is accompanied by lightning, avoid exposed places where you are taller than the surroundings.

Cold weather cycling is very invigorating. With the proper clothing and without rain and snow, it's even fun. I would much rather ride on a cold, crisp day in the winter than in a heavy wind on a summer day. Protection is a matter of choice and experimentation. Check the section in the Clothing chapter under Coldwear for some suggestions. Hands and feet can become numb in any weather, but in the cold it is crucial to keep them well covered. Because of pedal rotation and toe clip pressure, feet are especially vulnerable to wind chill.

If you run into snow on a tour, this is a

time when hitchhiking is justified. Thanks to the eruption of Mount St. Helens, the southern Oregon desert was thrust back to winter in late May in 1980. Usually the weather is dry and warm. However, we woke up in Prairie City with three inches of snow on our tent. Every direction had a mountain and each mountain was covered with snow. In addition, it was raining in the lowlands and a strong wind from the west further frustrated our efforts to escape the unpleasant environment.

We struggled west through John Day and Dayville, then turned north hoping for a reprieve from the wind if not the rain. At a Fresh Milk sign tacked to a tree by the road we stopped to rest and eat before starting over the snow-covered Blue Mountains. The old couple who sold the milk invited us into their cabin to warm up and insisted that we have toast and jam with our milk. After we were dry and full, they offered us a ride over the mountain. We accepted and were very glad we did after we saw what lay ahead. Daylight and our energy would have run out and left us near the top of the mountain where we would have spent a very miserable night.

# Dirt

As it was, our kind friend let us out above Heppner, we coasted down to a motel, crawled into the warm, dry double bed and watched color TV, wondering occasionally what all the poor cyclists were doing who were still trapped by the unusual weather.

Most of the time, if you're caught in wind and rain and snow, the worst you'll be is miserable. But misery can turn into hypothermia, and death can occur if the body temperature is lowered just six Fahrenheit degrees below normal. I prefer to be cautious and comfortable and compromise. I'd rather hitchhike, pay for a motel, and hang around laundromats than suffer or take a chance on a bad fall or hypothermia. Even the mildest symptoms demand immediate treatment. The ideal procedure is to submerge the victim in a tub of water heated to no more than 110 degrees Fahrenheit. If the warm water treatment is impossible, strip the victim and place him or her between warm, naked bodies in a dry sleeping bag. If conscious, the person should drink warm, lightly sweetened liquids such as tea with honey.

One of the many losses incurred by driving quickly over the land in a car is the awareness of different dirt road surfaces. A dirt road without sand, gravel, and washboards is a pleasure to cycle on. Even a rough road or trail may be well worth the effort because of the chance to explore the backcountry. Special places become accessible to the cyclist who is willing to ride such roads.

The Trans-America Trail has a few sections of dirt. There is no reason to be intimidated just because a road is dirt. Riding on dirt is more tiring to you and harder on your bike, but usually there's little traffic and the scenery is better. Plan longer rest stops and stop earlier in the evening. Adjust your expectations downward regarding speed per hour and miles per day. Relax and enjoy the country.

Usually it's very easy to see and hear traffic approaching on a dirt road. However, don't assume that cars will be where they usually are on a paved road. People like to drive down the middle of the road when it's dirt. You, too, will not want to ride in the far-right position but in a wheel track where the road is smoothest. Be careful when rounding a corner and on either side of the crest of a hill.

Touring exclusively on dirt roads or trails requires careful planning and equipment that's made to withstand rough conditions. Consult with professionals at bike shops and with other experienced cyclists. Wheels must be strong. At least use 27 by 1 1/4-inch tires. Heavy-duty, low-pressure tires (70 lbs.) are preferable to ones with a narrow bead and low rolling resistance. Perhaps you will need something as wide as 26 by 1 5/8- or 1 3/8-inch. Rims of box construction are stronger than other styles. Sealed bearings increase the chance of a trouble-free trip. But if they break down, you may be stuck for weeks. An alloy wire saddle or alloy racks may not be strong enough. Brazed-on fittings for racks and carriers are stronger than ones attached by nuts and bolts. In any case, fix screws and bolts with thread-locking compound and bring extra nuts and bolts. If anything can jar loose or fall out, it will. Several low gears, perhaps as low as 25, make climbing in

dirt easier. Fenders will keep the bike and rider cleaner. Goggles will protect your eyes from the dust. Each time you stop, check your bike. Trouble usually comes on slowly.

Backcountry bike camping, high biking, mountain biking, whatever you call it, requires self-sufficiency. Pre-trip study, detailed maps, extra water carrying capacity, plenty of food and protective clothing, more tools than usual and replacement parts may be necessary. Advise friends of your itinerary and don't count on being rescued if you get in trouble.

Bonnie Wong

96

# Night

The most important advice about riding at night on tour is to avoid it. When night falls, be in your tent sleeping. However, since the possibility of having to ride at night exists, always carry some kind of light with you. You can't always have my favorite lighting system, which is a full moon and dark surroundings, so a lighting system on the bike or rider is a necessary precaution. The road must be visible to the rider and the rider visible to other drivers.

A passive lighting system is merely reflective and includes tapes, clothing, and devices such as caution triangles, license plates, and reflectors that mount on the bike. Reflective articles can provide a lot of protection. Pedal reflectors, because of their movement, low placement, and yellow color, are easily visible. A three-inch standard trailer reflector mounted on the rear of the bicycle is brighter than any bicycle reflector or the common bicycle rear lamp. Front and side reflectors are not much use and side reflectors unbalance the wheel, even when mounted opposite the valve. They also increase the rotational weight of the wheel.

An active lighting system has lamps lit by generators or batteries. Red is the best color for rear lights or reflectors because red is the expected rear color. Headlights using three watts will be bright enough for normal speeds on normal roads. A low-powered (1.3 watts) battery lamp is adequate on dark roads at slow speeds. But when traveling at 15 to 20 mph (easy to do downhill) bicycle lights are inadequate because you won't be able to see most road hazards in time to stop. To be safe, don't ride fast at night. Leg lights are effective in making the cyclist visible because of their movement and low placement, but should be worn on both legs for optimum protection. Flashing lights will attract attention, but may confuse another driver, as their amber color is associated with road construction and emergency vehicles.

# Traffic

The bicycle is a vehicle and bicyclists should follow the same traffic rules as motorists. Ignorance and disobedience of traffic laws by cyclists hinders the acceptance of bicycling as transportation. In order to be safe and effective on the road, cycle with the rights and duties of a driver of a vehicle. Nearly all motorists cooperate with each other and typically they will cooperate with a cyclist as long as the cyclist acts in a reasonable and expected manner.

Cyclists who yield when they have the right-of-way create confusion and announce that their mode of movement is second class. Create "vehicular presence" for yourself; assume your rightful place, but with courtesy and caution.

**Wide and Narrow Roads.** The widest of all possible roads is the one with a wide, paved, smooth, clean shoulder, no matter how many lanes it has. That kind of a shoulder is shelter. Enjoy the freedom it provides, but watch for farm vehicles in rural areas. Don't ride on the far right side; ride nearer, but still to the right, of the shoulder line.

The narrowest road has no shoulder at all, or one that is cracked, graveled, littered, and, therefore, unrideable. It also has an outside lane that is too narrow to allow motorists to overtake cyclists in the same lane.

When the cyclist must share a narrow outside lane, the safest position is near the middle of the lane in order to be visible and to force traffic to slow down and pass with care. When the oncoming lane is clear for passing, pull over in your lane to give extra room to pass, but maintain a firm position on the road. If a car doesn't have to swing out and around you, it is likely to zoom straight by, cutting very close to your tender left side. The above procedure is a good general guideline, but it will not work well on narrow roads that are heavily used by trucks such as the infamous U.S. Highway 12 from Lewiston, Idaho, to Missoula, Montana.

The logging and grain trucks often cannot, but sometimes simply will not, pull out around a cyclist. The section from Kooskia to Missoula is part of the Trans-America Trail, but cyclists are not appreciated by the truckers. It's a matter of priorities. The grain and logs that are on the way to the ships and mill at Lewiston are business and there's limited space on the road. Bikecentennial has recently included a warning in their guidebook for that section: "Ride as far to the right as possible, wear very bright, visible clothing in addition to safety triangle, ride only in single file if in a group, get far off the shoulder when you stop, listen carefully for traffic behind you, and be prepared to pull off the highway." These are excellent general instructions for any narrow road that is heavily used. In this case, the better east-west route across Idaho may be the interstate, simply because the road is wider.

Sharing a lane can be fine when the lane is wide enough to allow a motorist to overtake within the lane and if the cyclist rides in a straight, predictable line. In a wide lane, ride two or three feet from the edge of the road, just inside the traffic lane. Since the lane is wide, the cars pass you by going slightly over the next lane line or the center line.

**Intersections.** Cars often come shooting out unpredictably onto the highway from country roads and driveways. A flange of gravel is often spread on the highway at intersections. Just because the road widens a bit at an intersection, don't move over to the far right. Motorists will assume that you are planning to turn and you may be forced off the road by a car turning right. Don't get stuck in a right-turn-only lane. Change lanes well before the intersection. Don't turn left from the right lane. Change lanes, looking behind you and signaling. If all else fails, you can become a pedestrian. Cyclists are unique in that they are the only drivers who can do that. It is usually safer and faster, however, to stay mounted.

**General Rules.** Never ride against the traffic. When the road has parked cars, intersections, cross-traffic or no shoulder, ride on the left of the right-most path to be in clear view of the traffic. When the road is clear of these conditions, move to the right, but still avoid the far right position. If traffic is heavy, communicate with other drivers. Indicate your desire to be let in or out of the traffic. When you are moving as fast as the cars, which happens going downhill, take a lane. Move over when you can't keep up with the traffic flow. Stay to the right if you're moving slowly. Watch out for cars that pull out of oncoming traffic to pass another vehicle. Many times they seem totally blind to the cyclist coming toward them. Time your crossing of narrow bridges so that both lanes do not have cars in them when you cross.

**Pollutants.** The irony of bicycling for one's health is that to do so, one must breathe automobile exhaust. Bicyclists, however, have a mobility in traffic that motorists don't have, and so can maneuver to avoid the worst. Avoid main streets anyway, particularly in summer and during rush hours. Also avoid industrial areas and take advantage of wind direction to reduce the inhalation of pollutants.

*What the motorist sees when cresting a hill.*

# Accidents

The most common cycling accident is falling, but the one that causes the most worry is the car/bike collision. Children and teenagers largely cause their own car/bike collisions, while motorist error is the main cause of adult collisions. Cyclists worry about being struck from behind, but 90 percent of all car/bike collisions are caused by conditions or actions that happen in front of the cyclist. Chances are that you won't get hit from behind if you can be seen and if you steer straight.

There are several situations in which the cyclist simply can't be seen and these require extra caution on the part of the cyclist. Ride far to the right when heading into, or away from, a low, setting sun, just over the crest of a hill, after a blind curve on the right, or if cycling unlighted at night.

Always be aware of the possibility of

having to leave the road. Think about where you would go and how you would do it. Learn how to stop quickly and make sudden turns in an emergency.

If you are assaulted by a motorist—run off the road, struck or hit with something—try to get the license number, the time and place and names of witnesses. It is important to bring a claim, civil or criminal, to collect on damages to yourself as well as to establish precedence for the prosecution of offending motorists.

If you are harrassed or threatened, write down the license number of the car so that the driver sees you. Get a description of the car and the driver. Flag down another car and ask them to call the police and have an officer sent to meet you. Wait for the officer in a safe place.

Certain types of drivers and vehicles consistently mean trouble. Watch out for pickups or "low riders," especially on weekend nights. Drivers of recreational vehicles and housetrailers often have little experience driving the monoliths they're piloting. Kids with puberty racing between their ears don't know any way to drive except fast. Old folks may hang timidly on your tail, afraid to pass.

Professional truck drivers, on the other hand, know how wide and powerful their rigs are. They are usually courteous and accommodating. They may not slow down, but they usually give as much room as possible when passing. Motorcyclists without exception have been friendly and helpful, or have ignored me, which is the response I prefer.

Certain constructions of metal and cement, certain arrangements of asphalt, plastic and glass, and certain entities of flesh and fur, are sources of considerable problems for cyclists. Drain grates in the gutter placed parallel instead of crossways to the traffic lie in wait for skinny tires. Diagonal railroad tracks trap narrow wheels. Manhole covers that rise above the road surface, potholes that drop, gaps between sections of the road, bridge joints, all can cause a serious wreck. The more moveable obstructions such as litter, cars, kids following balls, some dogs, and some drivers are equally dangerous.

What to do? First of all, pay attention to your driving. As the road is not prepared exclusively for you, you had better be prepared for it. Running into one parked car should be enough to teach anyone not to watch their rear derailleur shift, fascinating though it is. Try to get the city

to change the direction of the drain or sewer grates. If the tracks don't cross the street at a right angle, steer to a position which allows a right angle approach. In any case, slow down and coast over the most level place. Lift off the saddle, put weight on the pedals, keep arms and knees flexible. Cattle guards are placed perpendicular to the road, but cross them straight and slowly. Steer to avoid cracks, and gaps, and edges, and ridges. If caught between two surfaces or levels, don't try to climb out without steering to a right-angle position. Go very slowly.

Lift the front wheel up with a jerk over the far side of chuckholes and other differences in road surface such as between a driveway and the street. Avoid riding in the gutter because the rush of traffic sweeps trash there. Work for the passage of bottle deposit laws and support recycling programs. Look through the rear windows of parked cars for people and consider every person inside a possible door-opener. Allow enough room between your path and the parked cars for that possible open door. Ride in the traffic lane. Don't weave in and out around parked cars, and don't cycle closely behind parallel parked cars. Watch constantly for cars backing or pulling out of parking places.

# Dogs

If you see it or hear it far enough ahead, there will be plenty of time to read a dog's intentions and plan your strategy. Is the dog merely a protector, or is it an aggressor with expanded territorial claims? Most are only edge-of-property barkers and stay off the highway. Puppies tend to be dumb and get right under your wheels. These harmless animals I speak to in friendly tones, hoping to instill a positive regard for cyclists.

The ones that plan to attack, either by running you down or by lying in wait up ahead, have to be outrun, scared off, or negotiated with. Most of the dogs that chase are playful rather than vicious, but occasionally there is a truly mean one. On the level or downhill, outrunning is easy. A sharp and well-timed "No!" or "Bad dog!" will cause most to falter, if not stop. The voice of authority, no matter whose, speaks to their conditioned lobes. If

104

outrunning is impossible and confrontation seems certain, a squirt of water may shock them into retreat. The water bottle is an easier weapon to wield than a tire pump. Another trick is to pick up a beer can when approaching a dog-infested area. When the dog is several strides behind, drop the can in its path. The noise and the sight distracts the dog. By the time it has regained its wits, you are far gone.

A pack of dogs is a lot more trouble because together they plan to rule the world. If you are alone and unable to outrun them, you had better dismount, then talk and walk through their territory. When there's more than one cyclist, it is easier to deal with them because their attack is fragmented and they become confused, especially if everyone yells at once. It's one pack against another, and the dogs will usually back off because the cyclists are taller. It is a basically simple process of dogs and riders understanding each other's claims and purposes.

Flying insects can hardly be avoided. The ones that bite and sting are particularly perilous because it takes great self-control not to panic when you know that a wasp has just been swallowed up by your shirt and might embrace you before you stop and get your shirt off. Vast armies of gnats hatch out during summer evenings and ping off your helmet, face, arms and legs like little BBs. Don't cycle without some sort of eye protection.

On the first day of my first long trip, at the bottom of the first big hill, stood a bull. His horns spanned both lanes from his firm position in the middle of the road. Enormous, black, wide-eyed, he stared while I wrestled with the surprising and suddenly unwieldy bulk of me and my bike with its load. It was also the first day I had ever carried panniers. My back wheel began to skid. I eased up on the brakes, deciding that being close to the possibly peaceful bull was better than a sure dump on the asphalt. By the time I stopped, I could see the whites of his eyes. Straddling the bike, I stared back. What else to do? Tap him with my tire pump? Both of us wondered who would make the next move and what it would be. He flicked his tail and magnanimously trotted off the right-of-way, staring over his shoulder as I pedaled by, as fast as I considered to be polite.

# Discomfort

An accident probably won't happen, but certain discomforts probably will. For all the common discomforts, the first medicine is a change of body position. Raise or lower the seat, move it forward or back, change its tilt, change the position of the handlebars. It's possible that the frame is just too large for you or the saddle incompatible with your anatomy. If the frame is bent, even slightly, it is a struggle to keep it moving in a straight line.

Saddle soreness is the cyclist's lament. Easier to prevent than cure, and nearly impossible to avoid, a sore butt can be caused by either friction or pressure. Toughen up before leaving on tour by riding. Adjust the seat. On tour, pressure soreness can be relieved by a change of activity, such as walking. A rest stop every twenty miles or every two hours will prevent a lot of aches, pains, and grumbles. Shorts with a chamois or terry cloth insert add a layer of protection. Vaseline, talcum powder, and cornstarch are all used to prevent chafing from friction. I prefer to put the greasy stuff on the chamois and the powder on myself.

Sore knees is the next most frequent complaint. Tendons and ligaments all around the knee can be injured from the strain of cycling day after day. They can also become stronger. Heat applied locally and frequent massage will relieve the pain and speed the healing process, but healing after damage has been done is very slow. Tiger Balm or a mixture of cayenne and Vaseline are effective liniments. If your knees hurt, the first thing to do is to pedal in a lower gear. Next, change the position of your saddle. Also check the position of your feet over the pedals. The ball of the foot should be over the pedal spindle. Toe clips that are too long or short, or cleats that are improperly positioned, will cause knee pain.

Aches in the lower back, shoulder, and neck will often disappear with continued riding as strength increases. Remember that the body is plastic, not static. Be patient. Pain can be alleviated by massage, stretching, swimming, and soaking in hot water.

Numb hands are caused by nerve stress from road shock, pressure from body weight on the hands gripping the bars, and incorrect set-up between the seat and the handlebars. Using padded gloves, padded bars, and Randonneur bars, changing hand position frequently, and adjusting the saddle and handlebar position will help prevent numbness and tingling.

Numb feet are caused by interference with arterial circulation from tight shoes, tight lacing, toe clips, or straps. Lifting the leg momentarily on the upstroke restores circulation to the sole of the foot. It is one more reason to pedal "roundly."

There is no reason to suffer while riding a bike. There is also no reason not to push yourself occasionally to new levels of accomplishment, and that may involve some pain.

# The Blues

You can't dress to protect yourself from it, steer around or outrun it, but right alongside the external conditions that affect your cycling performance is how you feel. Some days that may be as vigorous as cold oatmeal.

So what to do? I get on the bike and ride anyway. An experienced tourist once advised me to ride for a couple of hours or twenty miles before deciding not to go any further that day. When I've arisen feeling low, I've followed his advice, and so far, have ridden out all my depressions. I have to push myself because I usually lead a sedentary life, and given a chance, lean in the direction of indolence. Maybe you don't.

Riding out the blues is different from taking planned rest days. Planning days of complete rest or low mileage will give your resumed cycling renewed enthusiasm— and help keep the blues at bay.

# EATING

For breakfast, find a bakery run by a Swiss family. Buy a croissant and a cup of coffee, sit in a delightful enclosed garden. Read the comics and the *Wall Street Journal* while you slowly chew and sip. No hurry. Thinking ahead, buy some bread and a jar of old-fashioned peanut butter. Later in the morning, stop along the road at a mom-and-pop roadside stand for strawberries to eat on the spot and for apples to carry with you. For lunch make peanut butter and whatever sandwiches. Try honey, bananas, applesauce, celery stalks, or cucumber slices. In the evening, gratefully accept an invitation to dinner and/or make one of your special dishes for everyone. Since you have the use of an oven, bake some yams and potatoes for tomorrow.

Next day, hit the local truck stop recommended by your hosts the night before. Hashbrowns, eggs, dark toast, apple pie, and coffee. On the road your nose catches a whiff of mint from the fields. Exploring, you find a crisp stand growing ditchside under a shady bridge. Pack some and relish the thought of mint tea some upcoming desert evening. By lunch, you have reached a town where cantaloupes are allowed to ripen on the vine. Eat one-and-a-half and catch your breath. Then a yam or two, carrots, and a peach for dessert. A simple, one-color meal. By dinner, you've reached the ocean. At a pungent, seaside market, buy crab meat, lettuce, spinach, cucumbers, and onions. Tear them up into a plastic bag and watch the sun set. Add olive oil and lemon juice and maybe dill. Gently place in pocket bread.

Breakfast the next day is leftover and mushy crab salad, its flavor deepened. Lunch is a saved and cherished cantaloupe half, very fragrant by now, filled with yogurt, bananas, and sunflower seeds, filled and refilled, and finally eaten with a squirt of lime juice. Dinner is something new. At the neighborhood deli in the last outpost of civilization, buy a slice or two of feta cheese, Greek olives, several hard rolls, tomatoes, and pickles. Make yourself a stack of sandwiches and eat one with a German beer. Rearrange your panniers and stuff in food because tomorrow's tour takes you to places where you won't even find a black banana, and where they haven't even heard of plain yogurt. Boiled sagebrush roots taste better than the coffee you'll find there. The bread would make a better napkin than a sandwich. You wish you'd brought a stove. You're awfully glad you didn't ride here just for the food.

Carbohydrates, fats, and protein in the food we eat become glucose, fatty acids, and amino acids. These nutrients, along with oxygen, reach the cells through the circulatory system. In the cells, ATP, a chemical compound, is produced from the combination of oxygen with glucose, fatty acids, and to a less extent, amino acids. ATP is the energy source for muscular contraction.

Carbohydrates are the food group comprised of simple and complex sugars— white bread to bulgur wheat, candy bars to apples. In the digestive tract, carbohydrates are converted to glucose (blood sugar), which can be used almost immediately to replenish the blood's glucose supply. Glucose is further transformed into glycogen, which is stored in the liver and muscles. When the blood glucose level falls below a certain point, the glycogen in the liver is rapidly converted into glucose and poured into the blood. This replenishes that which is consumed by ATP production in the muscle cells.

Carbohydrate stores are used to sustain strenuous activity. At such times, oxygen may be limited, but metabolism of carbohydrates can occur with and without oxygen. When the body has sufficient oxygen, both fats and carbohydrates are burned. Carbohydrates supply the energy for bursts of speed and concentrated power, but are stored in limited quantities.

Even in a lean athlete, there are about

# Good Food

thirty times as many calories of fat available for fuel as there are carbohydrates. Fat requires a great deal of oxygen to be metabolized, but as the body begins to run out of glycogen, more fats are burned. Fat stores, therefore, will sustain moderate activity for a long time. The fat supply is very valuable, but it does not need to be consciously built up or maintained as the carbohydrate supply does. A high-carbohydrate breakfast can be digested and stored in the cells ready for use in two to three hours. Fatty food requires about five hours to be digested. On tour, high-carbohydrate meals are the all-around best bet for energy.

Studies have been made that demonstrate the very high caloric consumption of hard-riding tourists. The best guide to eating, however, is to eat according to certain concepts: eat frequently, don't stuff yourself, avoid certain foods and emphasize others, and don't worry.

Naturally, you will want more energy than usual when touring. Naturally, you will eat more, but more is not necessarily better. Most of us have a tendency to look for any excuse to eat, and cycling 50 miles, day after day, is a good excuse. Before you grab and stuff, think about it. Are you really hungry? Is what's in your hand really good for your body? Really what you need?

I am 37 and become truly hungry only after exercise as vigorous as a long, hard ride. I love cycling for bringing back the childhood joy of appetite, but I don't need to eat twice as much on the road.

I do eat twice as often. Riding a bike all day, my body wants a constant supply of fuel, not a two-ton load of dirt and gravel all at once. It also wants a reliable supply of a certain type of fuel. I have discovered that I don't really want those foods which aren't food and aren't nutritious. When the body's voice is allowed to be heard, we discover that we are attracted to certain foods and repelled by others, and for very good reasons. Try not to assume "candy bar" when you hear your body yelling "quick energy." Interject banana. Get some juice. Both are high in potassium as well as fructose, a high-class sugar. A bike trip offers the opportunity to purify your body. Many veteran tourists will attest that wholesomeness as well as mountains can be survived.

When I'm touring, I mainly want food which has a lot of light in it, like fruit and vegetables. I also want many things which simply aren't available such as whole grains and tofu. While high in protein, tofu is still so rare in some places that it is considered a political statement. The cycle tourist is frequently at the mercy of bad restaurants and grocery stores with limited inventory. On the other hand, I've always been fond of a quotation I read somewhere to the effect that if a person is happy, rocks can be digested.

The point is to try to eat a low-saturated fat, high-carbohydrate, easily assimilated diet when touring. If you want a heavy meal, eat it at night when there is plenty of time to work with it. Eat light meals throughout the day. Avoid heavy doses of sugar and highly processed or greasy food. Generally, the closer a food is to the field or orchard, the better it is for you. Sodium and potassium supplements aren't necessary because there is plenty of sodium in food. The body maintains a balance between sodium and potassium. If you take salt tablets, then you won't have enough potassium. Aspirin and caffeine should be used moderately, if at all. Caffeine is diuretic, may cause stomach cramps, and an overdose becomes a stress rather than any sort of aid. Dairy products block absorption of

liquid and may be difficult to digest. Eggs are high in cholesterol. Meat contains no carbohydrates and is difficult to digest. A good diet should consist of about 55 to 65 percent carbohydrates. Paul de Vivie, father of bicycle touring, recommended eighty years ago in his "Seven Commandments for the Cyclotourist," that meat not be eaten while touring.

Whether you tour with or without a stove, food becomes your chief interest. Touring without a stove means you can simplify your day by eating what is available, what you find, and what you are given.

What's available is what's in the store when you are. Sometimes it's a choice between jerky, Twinkies, pig's feet, or pickles. Other times you can compose symphonies. There is fruit, especially the local and in-season varieties. But canned, unsweetened pineapple and applesauce are good when nothing is really fresh. I look for juice, vegetables, whole grain bread and crackers, cereals, yogurt, cheese, sunflower seeds, canned beans, pickled beets, green chili and hot salsa.

What's available is also what's on the menu. Breakfast is usually the least expensive meal to buy in a restaurant. Ask for honey packages instead of jam or syrup. A restaurant with a salad bar, even if it is not the best, means you can fill up for once on green and crunchy food. I always pick up a napkin or two and a couple of cracker packages. Health food stores, food co-ops, and farmers' markets stand out like oases in the desert.

Eating what you find is using wild food along the way. There are lots of watercress, chickweed, dandelion, berries, and old fruit trees. When cycling through Oregon and Washington in the late summer, you can't stop less than three times a day to savor the blackberries that grow profusely everywhere. What you find might be in tailored orchards. If someone is around I ask, if not, I eat the windfalls anyway. It is important not to trespass and

windfall-eating smacks of situational ethics. Gardeners are usually happy to sell or willing to give lovely, fresh sustenance. I've sometimes been tempted to snatch what I find leftover on the plates of restaurant customers before me.

Eating what you are given has been, for me, several home-cooked meals, milk just hours away from the cow, garden and orchard produce, fresh fish, several cold beers, and once, a shot at a town's potluck.

Stopping at cafes is a big part of the adventure for me, but cup after cup of the local brew is hard on the kidneys. I like to vary the coffee routine with cereal beverages, teas, and veggie broth. I can still observe the local life and pay for the privilege by paying for the hot water, or if I'm not charged, leaving the waitress the price of a cup of coffee and a good impression of cyclists.

A blend of herbs such as chamomile, catnip, and hops is relaxing. Sore muscles, unfamiliar surroundings, and an abundance of energy can interfere with much-needed sleep. A relaxing blend with pain-killing properties can be made with hops, lady's slipper root, wood betony, valerian, skullcap, and lobelia. The mixture can also be taken in capsules. Don't ride after drinking this mixture because it's a potent one.

Some tourists like to take vitamin and mineral supplements or perhaps caps of herbal mixtures. Hard riding increases the need for vitamins and minerals. Vitamin C and the B vitamins are water soluble and can't be stored by the body. They are the ones most easily lost when cycling and most commonly taken on tour. There is no danger of toxicity from taking C and the B-complex, as excess is eliminated in urine. Rose hips, cayenne, fruit, and sprouts are natural sources of C, and whole grain products and brewer's yeast are sources of B vitamins. Dark, leafy vegetables contain many vitamins and minerals. I have heard that it is possible to sprout alfalfa and wheat seeds in a plastic container fastened by cords or straps to the bike.

# Stove Cookery

In some bike camping situations, a stove is plainly a necessity, but most often it's a matter of choice, as it is easy to do without one in populated areas. To some, cooking adds to the enjoyment of touring; to others, it's a nuisance not worth the weight of a stove and fuel.

Traveling with children justifies cooking your own meals because quick, hot meals for youngsters are necessary for everyone's peace of mind. To keep my 11-year-old's spirits and glucose levels up, I promised him breakfast in a cafe, but lunch had to be bought in a grocery store and dinner cooked on the stove. If we were ten or fifteen miles away from a cafe in the morning, I fixed oatmeal which was quickly burned up by the ride to his promised pancakes.

Child or adult, it's an undeniable joy to have hot drinks in the morning and at night. Doing your own cooking reduces significantly the cost of eating, and more control over the quality of the food eaten is assured. Eating and cooking as group activites are a lot of fun.

Whereas backpacking requires the use of ultra-light and freeze-dried food, the menus of bicyclists can be nearly the same on the road as at home. Bought in the late afternoon and carried a few miles to camp, food can be canned, fresh, or frozen. Weight is barely an issue, especially with a group of hungry cyclists. The contents of a huge grocery bag can disappear in seconds into the panniers of several cyclists who are ready to find camp and eat.

Stoves using white gas (Coleman fuel), alcohol, and kerosene are refillable. One

can purchase white gas in gallons, alcohol in quarts, and kerosene often in bulk in the U.S. and almost anywhere overseas. Pressurized gas stoves (which use butane or propane) use fuel cartridges which must be thrown away when empty. The heavier stoves are the most stable. The best solution to group cooking, however, is two stoves, one for drinks and one for the main course. A couple of pots and a frying pan are enough cookware. The frying pans with a foldable handle and a Teflon coating are easy to pack and require less oil for cooking. A light pressure cooker is available from backpacking stores and would be worth its weight in

fuel savings for a group which is crazy about whole grains and beans. A lid can be used as a plate or a thin frying pan. Personally, I abhor light, thin cookware and prefer to use a heavier pot. Bring a spatula, a big spoon, some aluminum foil, and Ziploc plastic bags.

Remember to wash dishes away from watercourses. Soap isn't necessary. If you build a fire, use an established fire pit and dead wood. Keep the fire appropriate to your needs. Take advantage of the opportunity to cook and prepare food that can be carried with you the next day, like cookies or tortillas.

# Food to Carry

Whether you bring a stove or not, bring canisters, such as 35 mm film containers, of spices and herbs to help disguise or enliven restaurant and grocery store fare. A mixture of cayenne (or chili or curry), garlic powder, and basil (or oregano); a mixture of cinnamon, nutmeg, and cloves; and a mixture like poultry seasoning are basic. I also carry Ziploc bags of coffee substitute, teas, veggie broth, brewer's yeast, and sesame seasoning.

Brewer's yeast, high in B vitamins, tastes good on soups and salads. Sesame seasoning (gomasio) is made by roasting unhulled sesame seeds, grinding them in a blender or mortar and pestle, and adding salt and whatever you want in the way of flavoring, such as curry, dill weed, and thyme. The oil in sesame seeds turns rancid quickly after grinding and needs to be used soon.

Carry raw ingredients in strong plastic bags. You may want to mix ahead of time the dry ingredients of several pancake recipes or a cookie mix. For safety and

Bill Woolston

neatness, and to preserve the cook's sanity, put all the food in its own stuff sack. Perhaps the front panniers could be used exclusively as the kitchen end of the bike.

The following suggested foods are light, nutritious, easy to cook, and easy to carry.

**Seeds.** Sesame seeds are higher in calcium than milk and are also a source of zinc, potassium, and phosphorous. Careful toasting improves their flavor. It is better to grind them than to eat them whole. Chia seeds are very sustaining and a concentrated source of energy that is high in protein. Add to oatmeal and other grains. Sunflower seeds are also high in minerals. Toasting or cooking improves their flavor, but they taste good raw, too. Add to cooking grains and pancakes, or eat as a snack.

**Dried fruit.** If possible, buy the unsulphured kinds. Figs are high in magnesium and protein. Raisins are high in iron and carbohydrates. Dried fruit is a source of quick energy.

**Garlic.** Fresh or powdered, garlic is a body cleanser and tastes good.

**Soup bases.** Miso is a fermented paste derived most commonly from soybeans or barley and is a highly concentrated food. It has a salty taste, like bouillon. Add it to soups and stews at the end of the cooking. Make a clear broth by adding miso to hot water. Mix it with mashed beans for bean-spread sandwiches. Veggie broth is an instant soup mix that can also be used as a seasoning. Pea and lentil powders are a nearly-instant thick soup base. Pre-mix with garlic or onion powder and herbs. They can be combined with grain flours in bread and pancake recipes.

**Oil.** Cold-pressed, unrefined oils are the best. I also use olive oil on my skin instead of various creams.

**Flours.** Try flours such as rice, corn, soy, and rye as a change from wheat. They have different cooking and handling characteristics and can't be directly substituted for wheat in most recipes.

**Grains.** Whole grains and whole grain products are the very best sources of complex carbohydrates. Millet is the lightest and the quickest cooking of any unprocessed whole grain. Also try rice, rolled oats, farina, bulgur, and rice cream.

**Corn meal.** Use as a mush, in pancakes, or add to various batters. Adds a sweet taste.

**Granola.** Make your own. It is simple, nutritious, and filling.

**Baking powder.** The aluminum-free, single-acting type is best.

**Seaweed.** The various "sea vegetables" are light in weight and abundant in minerals. Kelp is an excellent source of sodium and iodine.

# Drink

"Water—the ace of elements," says Tom Robbins, author of *Even Cowgirls Get the Blues.*

You can cycle for a surprisingly long

distance on your stored fat, but without water, you won't get far. On desert days, I have lost track of the volume of liquid I have drunk—nearly two gallons, I suspect. That's eight quarts or thirty-two cups of water, juice, beer, coffee, or coffee substitute. And that doesn't count all the juicy fruit I could get my hands on like tomatoes, berries, melons, oranges, or grapefruit. You know you are using it when you drink all day long and pee only once.

When it's cold and damp, you may have to encourage yourself to drink. You can sweat a lot in cool temperatures, especially under plastic rain gear. "Drink before you're thirsty," is another of Monsieur Paul de Vivie's recommendations for cycle tourists. Always keep one water bottle filled and have another with you to fill for dry stretches, for climbing, or for heat. If you plan on camping away from civilization, carry an extra quart bottle in addition to your two water bottles. If used sparingly, two quarts will cook the evening meal, wash you and the dishes, and provide tea and breakfast.

There are many places where the water runs pure, but be judicious. Dysentery is a common ailment for cyclists. I have become very sick from drinking fast-running, icy-cold, crystal-clear water that had run through a cow pasture upstream out of my sight.

When I reach a grocery store and am both hungry and thirsty, I satisfy the thirst first by grabbing V-8 or apple juice, and then I shop leisurely and thoughtfully for food.

# RECIPES

Ordinary ingredients combined in more or less the same proportions in one recipe after another may not win awards, but will simplify cooking and carrying. The recipes are easy to remember, the food is easy to carry, substitutions are easy to make, and nothing will be damaged en route. Use of oil is kept to a minimum because oil is heavy. It improves flavor and texture, and helps get pancakes off the pan, but those qualities can be met minimally. Honey is heavy too, and a little goes a long way.

Tahini Candy, Sesame Treats, and Road Bread are suggested as things to make at home and carry with you. Pancakes and tortillas are extremely easy to make when camping. The rice dishes are also very simple, and quick-cooking rice can be used instead of brown rice to shorten cooking time. The recipes have all been tested on a variety of stoves, and some work better on one stove than on another. My advice is to try the recipes on your stove before leaving on tour. You can make adjustments in the ingredients and procedures to suit your tastes and equipment. Most simple one-pot meals (tuna casserole, spaghetti, and chili) are easily adapted for use on the road.

## Tahini Candy

1 c. rice flour
1/4 c. carob powder
1/4 c. coconut
2 t. brewer's yeast
1/2 c. ground or finely chopped dates
1/4 c. tahini

Mix thoroughly with hands and shape into balls. Chill. Can use other nut butters instead of tahini.

## Sesame Crisps

Carefully roast 3 c. of unhulled sesame seeds in a large pan over medium heat. Roast one cup at a time, stirring constantly. In a large bowl, mix together sesame seeds and some honey. Taste to determine if it is sweet enough. Press mixture into a pan. Chill. Cut into squares.

## Road Bread

4 c. of dry ingredients, such as 3 c. flour, 1/2 c. ground millet, and 1/2 c. rolled oats
1 t. salt
2 t. baking powder
1 c. water, milk, or juice
1/2 c. honey and molasses to taste
1/2 c. oil
1/4 c. seeds or nuts

Spread in a greased and floured 8-inch pan or several smaller ones. Bake about an hour at 300 degrees. Cool, cut into squares, air-dry for a while. It is best to mix the dry and wet ingredients separately and then combine without a lot of mixing.

## Taboulli

1 c. bulgur wheat
1/2 bunch parsley
1/2 bunch green onions
2 tomatoes
1/4 c. olive oil
1 lemon
1/2 t. salt
mint, hot peppers (optional)

Soak bulgur in water overnight or during the day for several hours. Drain. Add chopped parsley, onions and tomatoes, olive oil, lemon juice, salt, and mint and/or hot peppers if desired.
Serve cold if possible.

## Tortillas

2 c. dry ingredients such as 1 1/2 c. flour and 1/2 c. of cornmeal, or all flour, plus sesame or chia seeds
1/2 t. salt
3 to 4 T. oil
1/2 to 3/4 c. water

Knead. Pull off an egg-sized piece. Shape into a circular, thin patty with your hands, or roll out between plastic bags with a water bottle. Corn flour or corn meal makes a very sticky dough. You can add herbs or garlic. Brown (no oil) over fairly high heat until little dark spots appear. Turn. To put a filling inside, cook on one side, turn, place filling on cooked side, fold in half, cover, and steam. Turn to other side and continue to cook until filling is hot. Use cheese, cooked vegetables, or beans for filling. Smother with salsa. Turn down heat if the dark spots get too large.

## Enchiladas

Make separate piles of grated cheese, chopped onions and chopped tomatoes. Heat tortillas in foil or fry in a little oil, or hold over heat with tongs for a few minutes. Make a sauce of tomatoes, chili or cayenne, cumin, oregano, garlic, basil, and salt. Heat the sauce and soak the tortillas in it for a minute. Put the sauce-covered tortilla on a plate and sprinkle with onions, tomatoes, and cheese. Lay on another soaked tortilla and repeat. Top with beans.

## Corn Meal Cakes

2 c. cooked corn meal
2 c. chopped and grated vegetables
1/2 c. seeds
2 T. oil
1/2 t. salt

Shape into patties and fry until browned. Handles easier when cool. Carrots, parsnips, celery, and parsley are good vegetables to use. Sunflower, sesame, or chia seeds can be added.

## Fruit Soup

Soak dried fruits in apple juice overnight. Add fresh fruit and heat, or eat cold by serving over ice. Top with yogurt or a square of tofu. (It's not necessary to cook tofu.)

# CAMPING

The high point of the day may come when you are finally stretched out, flat at last. Finding a campsite begins, for me, with picturing what I want. Around four o'clock in the afternoon, I start imagining a secluded glade or meadow with water nearby. Sage steppe or fir forest, either are lovelier with a little juice to wash or swim in. For the next few hours, I watch for it. It doesn't always appear. Sometimes I find a perfect spot and pass it by because the riding is just too good to stop. I'll take my chances on down the road. Usually, I find some compromise between privacy and practicality, between the idyllic and the convenient.

About those chances on down the road: I've come close to being stuck a few times. Once, walking my bike through a deeply graveled stretch with a drop off on one side and a wall on the other, and night closer than any pavement, the only car in 30 miles picked me up. A sawyer took me right to a campground, said he'd been giving cyclists rides across that stretch of rock for ten years.

Another time, high on the Colorado prairie, the sun was sinking fast behind all the barbed wire and the cattle that surrounded me. Far ahead I saw a tiny white block on a green patch of nurtured grass. It was nearly dark when I asked if I could sleep on the lawn. The rancher insisted I make myself at home in a little teardrop trailer he used for hunting trips.

Floor space freely given is a pleasure to accept, but I would never go touring without shelter as close as my panniers. I carry a tent. It is comfort, security—and a bright, yellow sign. I don't always set it up. I would rather not be seen, and given a bugless, starry night with mild temperatures, I'd rather sleep in the open. I'm very happy to carry the weight of choice.

# Campsites

If it's flat and three feet by six feet, a cycle tourist can make a campsite out of it. In an area not "developed" for camping, a place to sleep may be a niche in the wilderness, a corner in a vacant city lot, or a picnic table in the town park. Such places may provide better sleeping and scenery than established campgrounds. However, finding such a place often takes a little extra time, effort, and presence of mind. It's a trade-off, sometimes a choice and often a necessity, because there are no campgrounds nearby. Part of the adventure and challenge of touring for me is to find a comfortable and free place to sleep. "Comfortable" means safe, as well as quiet, flat, and dry. In inhabited areas, finding such a spot may mean asking around, looking for a while, and even visiting the police station.

Small towns often allow camping in the city park. Usually, fires are prohibited and there is a limit on how long you can stay. If I'm cycling alone, I may tell a police officer where I'm sleeping. Other

possibilities for campsites are abandoned buildings, cemeteries, baseball diamonds, churches, backyards, and under bridges. Of course, to use any of these you have to make sure no one is living in the house, that ghosts don't bother you, that no game is scheduled, that you have permission, and that there is plenty of room for both you and any water that might come long. I have also slept in orchards, with permission, and harvested fields, without permission, and lots of other places where I couldn't ask because no one was around. In rural areas, exploring a dirt road that leaves the paved one is often productive. I always prefer to camp out of sight of all roads, even the little ones. I rest easier with just animals and birds knowing my whereabouts. I aim to be minimal and very polite.

Campgrounds in national parks and forests, and provincial, state, or private lands can be very satisfying. They may offer security, companionship, and attractions of special interest and beauty. Level places abound, water is usually abundant, clean, and sometimes even pumped through a shower. Beating clothes clean on rocks in a cold stream has its merits, but so does a sink with hot water and soap. A picnic table is one of my favorite campsites. I can watch the stars wheel, yet the bed is flat and off the damp ground. If it is under a roof, let it pour outside. I'll be dry and so will my tent and bike.

Campground fees vary, but whatever they are, they're usually cheaper for the camping cyclist than the camping motorist. A group of cyclists sharing one or two tents can also share the cost of the camping fee. The solo cyclist usually cuts such a low profile that he or she may be ignored. When I'm traveling alone, I scout around campgrounds for a place as far away as possible from the mainstream of car campers. I feel safer on the fringes of facilities than in the middle of them. Since I don't bother with a fire, may not even cook or set up a tent, I seldom take a regular, numbered campsite. When I camp in a busy campground, I usually visit my neighbors. I like to know who's sleeping next to me. Fellow campers can be sources of information about the

# Selection

In selecting a campsite, remember the purpose is to rest, not to rearrange the scenery. Wherever you are, adjust yourself to the landscape. Camp so that no one can tell you were there. As Harvey Manning says, "Take only pictures and leave only footprints." Look for a flat spot, a dry spot, and a warm spot, out of the wind and where the sun will hit you in the morning. Sleep on dirt or grass rather than on flowers. A breeze will blow the mosquitos away. Stay back from watercourses. Don't build fires unless it's necessary for cooking, drying, or warming. Leave the trees alone. Use only dead wood for fuel. Replace what you had to move in order to set up camp, and pack out all garbage. Whether you are in the wilds or on a soccer field, leave the site clean and repaired.

If you don't feel safe in a place—urban, rural, or forested—then move, even if you are set up, very tired, and a rational adult. If you have a creepy feeling about your selected campsite, don't talk yourself into staying there. General awareness is heightened by the freedom and exercise of cycling. Pay attention to your inner voice. Under the best conditions, it may be difficult to fall asleep. Every muscle is tired, but the miles are still flying by, your ears are still roaring, and your legs pumping. You should be able to enjoy the increased awareness cycling brings and not worry about your safety at night.

Don't forget to lock your bike if there is any chance it might be stolen.

road ahead and can also be entertaining company. A fire seems more justifiable when it's shared by several people. Travelers thrown together by circumstance can be scathingly honest about themselves and about you. Unforgettable confessions are breathed to the fire-lit night. Stories, memorized poetry, music, games, and songs make camping with others—friends or strangers—a rich and treasured experience.

If you arrive at a commercial campground too late to get a site and too late to look any more, ask someone already set up to share his place and fee with you. Several campgrounds I have stayed in have "hiker and biker" areas. The fee for these undeveloped campsites is nominal and voluntarily paid. I certainly would like to see more of this kind of development.

# Lodging

When every item in your bags is soaked, you are filthy, sore and sick to death of natural living, buy yourself some ease. A hotel room is then worth every bit of the cost. Most of us can rough it out for short periods of time, but rain, snow, wind, two passes or five flats in a day will wear on the toughest veterans. A youngster may really need the comfort of a room and bed. Besides, it can be a lot of fun.

Most small towns will have an old hotel with worn carpets, creaking stairs, musty halls, and low rates. A small family-run motel is often clean and cheaper than the big-name chains. Don't overlook the possibility of renting a motel room for a few hours during the day, simply to shower and rest. Day rates are usually half price.

Hostels are well worth their small cost. Many people across the country have opened their homes to passing cyclists (see the References section at the back of this book).

# Waters

Once you have made your sleeping arrangements, the empty evening will stretch before you like the stocking on Christmas Eve, flat with promise. Flat as your belly. Maybe you should eat, or eat some more. If you've already eaten, or are more dirty than hungry, your concern after finding a campsite is probably water. Food and water are the continents and seas of the cyclist's world.

Public swimming pools and university gyms offer bountiful hot and cold water. Athletic clubs will often sell, or even give, a shower and sauna to a tired-looking cyclist. Various establishments with public restrooms supply the opportunity to hit the high spots, as my mother used to say.

Oceans, lakes, reservoirs, and streams offer the ideal way to conclude a cycling day. Swimming makes you long and lean again after hours of muscle-shortening riding. Soaking in a hot spring will set every cell aglow. When planning your tour, locate any hot springs along the way. They are worth the extra miles off your route to get to them.

# Massage

Keep moving after you get off the bike. With or without water to play in, sore or not, keep moving. Metabolic end-products stagnate in still muscles and breed aches that really hurt by morning. Go for a walk and explore your surroundings, in town or in the country. Give yourself a massage, or trade a massage with a companion. Massage helps remove the by-products of muscle contraction and sends them into the circulatory system to be eliminated. If you carry one book with you, let it be a massage book. Or learn a simple procedure ahead of time.

Massage can actually help strained muscles heal and prevent subsequent strain, as well as ease pain. The mind and body will be relaxed for sleep after a massage whether you give it to yourself or receive one from a friend. Even giving a massage can be relaxing. Shiatsu massage lends itself perfectly to a camping situation as neither oil nor the unclothed skin is necessary. Only warm hands and a good heart, said a shiatsu teacher of mine. Shi (fingers) atsu (pressure) is an Oriental system of diagnosis and treatment based on the belief that health is a matter of balance within the body. The technique of shiatsu has risen from the simple observation that our natural reaction to pain is to place the hand on the area that hurts and press it. Pressing on particular points improves the flow of energy through the body. Pressure is often initially painful, but eventually the pain is relieved.

Bill Woolston

# Stretching

Some cyclists prefer to stretch right after riding, some before. In any case, stretching and loosening are important. I usually stretch in the morning when my muscles seem two inches shorter than usual and I'm as stiff as an old shoe. I have developed a set of slow movements that take from ten to twenty minutes to go through, depending upon how long I hold each position and how many of them I do.

The whole sequence works generally from the top of the body down and stretches every muscle. Included in my routine are up and down torso stretches (done while standing), neck rotations, spinal twists, rolling on my spine, shoulder stands, the infamous yoga plow, several leg stretches, and Tai Chi moving sequences.

Exhale while bending forward and breathe slowly while holding the stretch. One position should be connected to the next without abrupt breaks. No bouncing, gasping, or grunting allowed. No deep knee bends. If a stretch is too easy, there will be no gain in flexibility. If the stretch is too long, injuries can occur. Many exercises can be done with another person and the stretching that results seems extra profitable.

Learning a set of stretches and some massage procedures are part of the training process for a long ride. These skills may not be as necessary as being able to bike day after day, but they are very helpful in achieving mileage goals.

Bonnie Wong

# Equipment

You can buy a room, accept a spot of floor space, sleep in a stand of pines or headstones, recline on an air mattress in a tent, or roll up in an army blanket on the ground, but it remains that one person's shelter is another's suffering. What you protect yourself with in repose—tent, bivvy sack, tarp, or just a pad and bag—depends upon your standards for comfort, the conditions you expect to encounter, how fast you plan to ride, and, as always, on what you are willing to spend.

My personal response to rain and mosquitos requires me to carry a tent—a double-wall, true tent—in order to be comfortable. I am willing to spend a lot of money to stay dry without having to haul much weight. In a bivvy sack, however, I think I would feel exposed and trapped, like a slug on a sidewalk in a rainstorm. If a route of mine should ever lie through warm lands rarely lapped by rain, I would surely gear down to a bivvy sack, or a tube tent, or just a bag and pad—protection appropriate to the need.

Temperatures on a summer tour that includes mountains or seacoasts will probably not fall below 30 degrees Fahrenheit, at least, not often. Chances are the temperatures won't be too low for comfort if your equipment is minimally adequate and your standards match your gear. Remember, a warm and dry night's sleep is a night's rest, but a cold and wet night's sleep is just a night's miserable passing.

# Tents

A bike camping tent does not need to be as elaborate or strongly built as a mountaineering tent, and can thus be constructed of lighter and less expensive materials. The primary considerations are weight and rain protection. As a general rule, shelter weight should be between three and four pounds per person. The less weight, the less protection and living space. Though rain protection is only one purpose of a tent, it is the most difficult to attain.

A true tent consists of an inner tent of lightweight, breathable, uncoated nylon, a floor of tough, waterproof, coated nylon, and a rainfly of coated, waterproof nylon.

The two-part construction is cool in hot weather as well as dry in wet. Another design employs only one layer of a waterproof but breathable material such as Gore-Tex. Ventilation, shape, and ease of setting up are also very important. For wet weather touring, a design which allows window and door to be kept open for greater ventilation (a tunnel canopied at both ends) is the best. The quality of the materials, including poles and pegs, is an indication of the quality of overall workmanship.

I was fortunate enough to buy a used tent that I consider perfect for my bike camping needs. It keeps me dry, weighs

three pounds, takes five minutes to assemble and disassemble, is shaped charmingly like a tunnel and is a cheery yellow. The only drawbacks to my cherished summer palace are two: it's expensive if you buy it new, and the nylon is so light that I fear it will not last long.

Tube tents, commonly made of polyethylene, are erected with a length of cord tied between two well-spaced trees. The sleeper holds down the floor. Open at the ends, they provide protection only from weather and insects that arrive vertically.

# Tarps

A tarp above protects against vertically falling rain and hot sun, but not against slanted rain, wind, or bugs. A tarp below serves as a ground cover. For minimal cost and weight, a tarp provides minimal shelter. Made of polyethylene, reinforced polyethylene, or best of all, urethane-coated nylon, a tarp can be shaped according to what you need and what there is to tie onto. Lightweight poles can be carried for supports.

An A-tent is made by tying a cord between two trees, draping the tarp over the cord and staking the corners. Another design is made by tying the grommet in the center of one of the sides to a tree four or five feet above the ground, and staking the two corner grommets on either side of the tied-up center. The other two corners are pulled back and staked. This shape has a high front door and zero clearance in the rear, but it does have sides. A shed-roof design is made by staking the back grommets and tying front grommets to trees or rocks several feet above the ground.

Ground covers can be as cheap and thin as cleaners' plastic, or as durable as coated ripstop or nylon taffeta. Their purpose is simply to keep wet, dirty, and sharp things from penetrating your tent floor, pad, or sleeping bag. Coated nylon can be bought from fabric stores and sewn into a shape slightly smaller than the tent floor. Otherwise, when the rain washes down the walls, it can flow between tent floor and ground cover and create a water bed. Remember to seal the seams. I've used a plastic poncho as a raincoat, bicycle cover, and ground cover.

# Bivvy Sacks          Bags

Bivvy sacks hold a sleeping bag, a pad, and usually one sleeper. The simplest sack is an envelope with a waterproof bottom, a breathable, uncoated top, and no hood or bug netting. It won't keep you dry in the rain. The more complicated sack has a hood, netting, a Gore-Tex top, and a Gore-Tex or other waterproof bottom. Special materials aside, the design is crucial in providing protection from water, so seams must be sealed. Bivvy sacks are feather weights (16 to 26 ounces) and can be rolled up into a five- by ten-inch package.

An additional advantage is that bivvy sacks allow you to sleep in places where a tent or tarp can not be set up—in heavy forests and deserts and under bridges.

Four inches of loft (1 1/2 pounds of down or 3 1/2 pounds of polyester) in a sleeping bag should provide enough warmth at any temperature above freezing if you, your bag, and your clothes are dry and out of the wind, and if your head is protected.

Take the time to study thoroughly the different designs, constructions, and materials used in sleeping bags if you plan to buy a new one for bike touring.

Notice the bag's overall shape, provisions for head protection, insulation, shell materials, zippers, stitches per inch, draft tubes, and containment of insulation.

Buy the smallest bag that fits comfortably. Differential cut (smaller on the inside) is considered warmer by some. More important is to start with a well-filled bag of high quality workmanship. As a shell material, nylon taffeta is stronger, more abrasion-resistant, and more down-proof than ripstop nylon. It is also more expensive and heavier. A liner of polyester, cotton, and nylon blend eliminates the icy feeling of pure nylon.

Insulation creates a thermal barrier of still air. The synthetics are less affected by

*Overloaded in the rear.*

moisture, provide warmth when wet, are a uniformly dense barrier, but compress less than down. Down is still the best insulator per pound, but the quality of down varies. Most down bags have internal walls or baffles of either a box, slant box, or V-tube design. A sidewall baffle is necessary to keep down from migrating footwards. Quilting or sewn-through construction leaves no insulation at the seams. Synthetic fillers do not require elaborate interior construction to keep the insulation in place. Designs combining down and synthetics are available, with the synthetic on the bottom and the down on the top for greatest warmth.

Liners and overbags, socks and wool hats, or having more than one body inside a sleeping bag or tent greatly increases warmth. Two people don't necessarily need two bags. With good insulation underneath, such as air mattresses, pads, or sheepskins, one big sleeping bag opened to cover two people like a quilt may provide plenty of warmth.

The catalogs of outdoor suppliers contain much information about the fabrics, insulators, construction techniques, and designs of outdoor clothing and other equipment used for camping. Study them before choosing equipment for your bike tour.

# Pads

Pads add a lot of insulation for little weight and trouble. Open-cell foam pads must be thicker than the closed-cell kind in order to provide the same amount of insulation, but they do provide a softer bed. A short, narrow pad from hips to shoulders is sufficient and saves space. The closed-cell pads, such as ensolite, are waterproof and less bulky. Open-cell pads need to be covered if there is a chance of rain. Air mattresses are heavier than either type of pad, but there are some types which offer a great deal of comfort for little weight, bulk, and bother.

Sheepskins are very warm and comfortable, although heavy. A child on a fleece in a tent may be warm enough with just a blanket as a cover.

Diana Armstrong

# First Aid, Etc.

With the following items, you may not be ready for an emergency, but you should be prepared to take care of the most common road complaints.

- Band-Aids, tape, gauze pads, elastic wrap, moleskin
- Witch hazel for cleaning scrapes, soothing itches and bug bites
- Olive oil and aloe vera for burned, dry skin

- Lip balm, sunscreen, zinc oxide
- Bug repellant
- Multi-purpose biodegradable soap for shampoo, body, and dishes
- Corn starch or baby powder for your bottom and also to smooth over tube patches. Vaseline can be used instead of powder (but not on the tube!)
- Tiger Balm (or cayenne powder to mix with petroleum jelly for a sore-muscle salve)
- Baking soda for bites, sunburn, washing, and toothpowder
- Sunglasses are very important. The greater their capacity to shade, the better they will be for touring. Foam cushions on the nose and ear pieces increase comfort.

Other important items are safety pins, needle and thread (dental floss can be used as thread), matches, flashlight, towel (a diaper is very absorbent, light, and smaller than a regular bath towel), lock and cable, and identification. A camera, log book, pen, stamps, and a note telling whom to contact should you meet your Maker might be included. Halt, or something similar, will stop potential assaulters and other dogs. Kitchen equipment is discussed in another section of this book, but a bowl or cup, spoon, knife, and can opener are probably essential. Ziploc bags are convenient for carrying leftovers and soft fruit bought on the road. A very lightweight day pack or net bag is handy for transporting to your campsite food bought in the late afternoon.

# REPAIRS

Take precautions rather than make repairs. Keep your personal experience with roadside repairs minimal by starting with a perfectly adjusted machine and enough knowledge to maintain it. Attempt to be self-sufficient, to own and to know how to use the tools required to maintain your bike. At least, understand the principles involved.

Before my first tour, I had visions of my ball bearings springing from their races at some predetermined distance from the nearest bike shop, say 200 miles, and the road being deserted under pouring rain and approaching darkness. Luckily, my fears were unfounded. A well-built, properly assembled, carefully maintained bike, correctly loaded and properly ridden, should supply trouble-free service for many, many miles. I average a flat tire and a broken spoke every 1000 miles.

Once, the cable to the rear derailleur pulled out of the cable clamp bolt when I was standing up and cranking hard over a small hill. I was promptly thrown to the pavement. A little dazed and scraped, I moved to the side of the road, furious with myself because I had known the night before that the bolt was loosening but had forgotten about it in my rush to find a cup of coffee somewhere. Sponging my knee with witch hazel and rubbing my head, I berated myself for my foolishness. Just then, a cyclist appeared on the crest of the hill behind me. He had the needle-nosed pliers I needed for the job. In another ten minutes, we were off, looking for the mythical bakery of every touring cyclist's early morning dreams.

The law of broken spokes is that they always break on the freewheel side of the rear wheel because then you have to take everything apart to replace them. I have broken one in the front and one in the rear on the non-freewheel side. I know my number is up. That's why I am collecting more tools and the knowledge to go with them. Beginner's luck may be renewable, but it's not a permanent condition.

An experienced bike mechanic has savvy with tools and a feel for miniscule adjustments that I don't have. I understand how my bike works, but I lack a lot of ability when it comes to making major repairs and doing the fine tuning that is so important on a good bike. I like to work on my bike and intend to continue learning about it, but I don't mind paying for expertise.

# Tools

The number of tools you carry bike camping depends upon your knowledge, the availability of assistance, length of tour, and severity of the terrain and conditions. The list that follows is more than adequate for a tour through the United States or Canada, and any country where ten-speed touring is common.

- For wired-on tire repair: two levers, tube, patch kit, repair canvas, piece of tubular tire or duct tape, a metal valve cap with a tighener on top for Schrader valves
- Screwdriver, 1/8-inch blade
- Chain remover tool and spare links
- Allen wrenches that fit your bike
- Some small wrenches or a "Y" wrench with 8, 9, and 10 mm sockets or sockets that fit your bike
- Extra spokes and nipples (three to twelve), and a spoke wrench. Tape extra spokes to the rack support.
- Freewheel remover and 8-inch adjustable wrench
- Lubricant
- A few nuts and bolts, especially the sizes for racks and fenders
- Needle-nose pliers (optional)
- Strong twine to use as a third-hand tool when adjusting brakes and for use as a clothesline (optional)
- Shift and brake cables (optional)
- Cleaning rag, toothbrush (optional)
- Brake blocks (optional)

# Daily Check

Each day, give your bike a tender going-over. Check the *tires* for imbedded glass and thorns, and battered cords. Give them a little air. Squeeze the *spokes* to check tautness and to locate any broken ones. Check the truth of the *wheels* by spinning each wheel and watching as it passes between the brake blocks. If you want a more precise test than simple eyeballing, hold a pencil near the moving rim and watch for any change in distance between the rim and the point. Since the trip should have started on well-built and tuned wheels, they should remain true unless you break a spoke or crash. Hitting a lot of bumps on well-built and tuned wheels won't necessarily compromise their truth.

A well-tuned wheel has virtually uniform spoke tension and uniform spoke sound (about A-sharp above middle C). The spokes are laced and no spoke threads should show below the nipple. The rim has lateral truth, is round, and centered over the hub of the wheel in front and the axle in the rear (which is halfway between the dropouts in both cases).

Check the *brakes*. If they are loose, tighten them by raising the barrel adjusters on the cables or by tightening the cables. Cables stretch with use, particularly the new ones. A third-hand tool (you already have the first two hands) squeezes the brake calipers together to allow pulling the cable tighter. It can be made by wrapping a piece of twine back and forth between the two brake block bolts. Check the brake pads for alignment with the rim. They should be about 1/32-inch below the top of the rim.

Lubricate the *chain* every other day or every third day, depending upon the conditions and the type of lubricant. In wet weather, lubricate more often. A chain lube is a heavier oil in a lighter carrier. Several lubricants commonly used on bicycles are available in small containers, perfect for touring. WD-40 is very light and should be used more often than something like LPS-3. Tri-Flon is a synthesized, non-petroleum-based lubricant that carries Teflon-like particles. It lasts longer in wet conditions than LPS-3, which lasts longer than WD-40; but WD-40 is acceptable if used daily.

A lubricant that is sprayed on the chain will wash grit out, but a lubricant that is dripped out of a bottle or cartridge is neater. After lubricating the chain, wipe off the side plates to prevent the oil from collecting dirt. Wipe the rims free of oil and dirt so that the brakes will operate at peak efficiency. Whenever necessary, also spray or drip thin to medium weight lubricant on the rear derailleur jockey sprocket and tension roller. Remove the chain from the derailleur cage, if possible, and twirl the rollers. Lubricate the derailleur pivots and the brake pivots. On sidepull brakes, the pivot is the same bolt that mounts the brake to the frame. On centerpulls, there are two pivot points, one above each shoe. Also lubricate the brake lever pivots, the shift levers, and the pedal bearings. Wipe everything off after lubrication.

The housings and cables should be greased before leaving on tour and shouldn't need any attention on the road. If the freewheel has to be removed in order to replace a spoke, clean and oil it. To clean it, use a rag to remove grease from between the cogs. Within a shallow pan, hold the freewheel at an angle. Slosh clean solvent over cogs and scrub with toothbrush. Wipe dry. Lay flat on paper or rag and drip oil into body. It also can be oiled on the bike. With the wheel on its side, drip oil in the seam while twirling the cluster around the stationary freewheel body until the action is smooth and the sound muted. Oil rots rubber, therefore wipe off the rims, tires, and brake blocks. While lubricating, check the nuts and bolts, which can vibrate loose.

Before beginning another day's adventures, make sure the panniers are fastened and everything is battened down tight. Lots of stuff that you planned to put in last gets left on rocks and logs.

Happy cycling! Bon route!

# Trueing
# a Wheel

- Determine the length of the bulge in rim as it passes between brake blocks.
- Hold onto the spoke at one end of the bulge and place the spoke wrench on the spoke at the other end of the bulge.
- Looking down at the wheel, if the bulge is to the left, tighten the spokes that go to the right side of the flange and loosen the spokes that go to the left. If the bulge is to the right, tighten the spokes that go to the left flange and loosen the ones that go to the right.
- The rim will gradually move over and the bulge will disappear.
- Tighten by turning clockwise, looking down at the wheel, a quarter-turn at a time. A one-eighth turn should be made if the bulge is slight, and at the beginning and end of the bulge where it tapers out.

# Changing a Tire

To remove the wheel from the bike, release quick-releases on brake and hub, or unscrew bolt-on style hub. If you are removing the rear tire, put the chain on the smallest freewheel cog, pull derailleur back all the way, and push forward on the wheel.

Taking a wired-on tire and tube off the rim:

- Let remaining air out of the tube.
- Insert the tire lever under the tire bead opposite the valve hole.
- Hook the other end of lever to the most convenient and nearest spoke.
- Insert another tire lever about two inches to one side of the first.
- Release the first lever and insert it again about two inches on the other side of the second lever.

- Release the second, and carefully pull lever towards you, sliding bead out of the rim all the way around.
- Pull tube out, starting at the opposite valve hole.
- Pull the valve out of the valve hole and set the tube aside where it won't get dirty.
- Pull off the other bead from the rim.

Putting the tire and tube on the rim:

- Place one bead of the tire onto the rim.
- Put enough air into the tube to make it round.
- Put the valve through the valve hole in rim strip and rim.
- Tuck the tube into the tire all the way around.
- Move tire and tube assembly over and above rim.

- Push valve up into the tire so the second tire bead can seat on the rim.
- With both hands, push the bead onto the rim, working around the rim away from the valve.
- When you get near the end, where it gets tough to push the bead in, let some air out of the tube. Squeeze hard with your thumbs or the heels of your hands. A new tire can be very tight, but an older one should snap on without much trouble.

Check to make sure the tire is evenly seated all around the rim. Squeeze the tire and look to make sure the tube is not caught under the bead. Make sure the valve is perpendicular to the rim. If it is not, you must re-position the tube so that the valve projects from the rim at a right angle.

Pump air in the tube. Grasp the pump barrel with your fingers and wrap your thumb around the tire to support the pump on the valve. Don't twist Presta valves. Support the left elbow on the left thigh if you are right-handed.

# Fixing a Tube

The very first thing to do when you have a flat is to check the tire while on the bike for a nail, sticker or glass. If you find it, remove the wheel, mark the spot and remove just that part of the tube which needs to be patched. You can fix the tube on the wheel. If you can't find what caused the flat, check the valve. Loosen it and tighten it down again. Pump the tire up and wait to see if it now holds. If the tire continues to lose air, do the following:

- Remove the tube and tire.
- Locate the puncture by pumping the tube up until it is tight, and listen or hold it to your cheek to feel the air-flow.
- When you find the hole, use sand-paper to roughen the area around the puncture.
- Clean the area thoroughly to remove dirt, grease, and rubber particles.
- Put glue around the puncture and let it dry until it's tacky.
- Burnish down the patch on the glue with a tire lever.
- Rub baby powder over the patch.
- If you don't know what caused the flat, run your fingers all over the inside of the tire as if you were feeling fabric. If you can't find anything, check under the rimstrip for a spoke that may have worn a hole in the tube by protruding above the nipple. Something caused the flat; find it.
- Make sure the valve is snug on the new or repaired tube.

# Fixing a Tire

# Cleaning the Chain

If your wired-on tire is only punctured, don't worry about it. And if it is slashed with glass, it can be repaired. For a slashed tire:

- Remove the tube and the tire.
- Put either a piece of old tire with beads cut off or a piece of tubular tire on top of the slash on the inside of the tire. A piece of canvas cloth coated with rubber cement, adhesive tape, or even a Band-Aid can serve the same purpose.
- The air pressure of the tube will hold the "boot," or patch, in place.

If the tire is badly slashed, and you have no spare, you can still ride it to civilization. Inflate tube partially (soft), and tape tire to rim with electrician's tape. First-aid adhesive tape can also be used. It may even look more appropriate, to fit the injury.

Now inflate the tire to near normal, depending on how large a slash and how it holds. This is an emergency measure, and make sure not to apply a brake to that tire.

Chains are worn out if they make a lot of noise going over the teeth of the smallest rear cog, especially when you pedal hard. If daylight can be seen under three links when you grasp one link and pull the chain away from the large chainring, the chain is stretched out. Twenty-four links of new chain measure 12 inches. If 24 links measure 12 1/8 inches, the old chain is still okay, but if 24 links measure 12 3/8 inches, you need a new chain. Cycling with a worn-out chain wears down the teeth on the small rear cog in particular. Shifting becomes more difficult, too. If a new chain is bought, measure it against the old one to determine the number of links needed for your bike.

# Replacing a Spoke

It is possible to do a fairly good job of cleaning the chain with it still on the bike, but it is easier and more thorough to remove the chain to clean it.

- With a chain tool, push any pin most of the way out by twisting a half-turn at a time. Count turns—six for a 3/32-inch chain. Be careful not to push the pin out of the far sideplate.
- Bend the chain at the pushed-out pin to separate the link.
- Soak the chain in kerosene or thinner.
- Brush all four sides of the chain.
- Swish the chain again in kerosene and wipe it dry. If you have the time, let the chain air dry.
- Replace the chain around the chainring and rear cog.
- Push the pin carefully and squarely back into position.
- Make sure the pin sticks out an equal distance from both sideplates.
- Stress the chain to make sure the link moves freely. Some chain tools have a slot to use for seating the pin.
- Lubricate the chain.
- Wipe sideplates to remove excess lubricant.

Spokes break from improper tension, either because they are too loose and flexing at the elbow, or because they are too tight and pulling out of the threads. If you break a spoke and cannot replace it right away, loosen the brake so the rim doesn't rub the break pad. Continue riding until you can get the spoke replaced.

To replace a spoke on the front wheel or rear wheel, non-freewheel side:

- If the spoke broke at the elbow, unscrew the old spoke from the nipple.
- Try to screw the new spoke into the old nipple.
- If it fits, unscrew it, thread it through the hub flange hole, lace it properly, and screw the nipple down over the spoke threads.
- If it doesn't fit, or if the spoke broke at the nipple, remove the wheel, tire and tube. Lift up the rimstrip, remove the old nipple, put the spoke through the hub flange hole, then lace and screw the new nipple down over the spoke.
- Make sure you have put the spoke through the hub flange from the correct direction and have laced it properly.
- Tighten the spoke to the same tension as the other spokes.

On the rear wheel, freewheel side (for most, but not all, hubs):

- Remove the wheel.
- Remove the freewheel.
- Install the extractor (freewheel re-mover) using the quick-release mechanism to hold the extractor in place.
- Install an 8-inch adjustable wrench on the extractor, making sure it is on tight.
- Stand the wheel up and lean it against something with the freewheel side on your right and the adjustable wrench parallel to the ground, the handle towards you. Holding the wheel firmly with your left hand, press down hard (but with finesse) on the wrench with your right foot. That is, move the freewheel extractor in a counter-clockwise direction as viewed from the freewheel side of the wheel.
- Remove the quick-release mech-anism.
- Unscrew the freewheel. It comes off as a unit.
- Replace the broken spoke as you would for the front wheel.
- Oil the threads and replace the free-wheel, being very careful not to cross-thread it.
- Secure the freewheel. Pedaling action will tighten it further.

# Photographer's Notes

There is probably no other physical exercise and mode of transport which lends itself to photography as well as bicycle touring. The extra weight of a camera with one or two lenses is seemingly negligible as you cruise along. On other occasions, when the hills are endless and the heat insufferable, your 35mm camera will provide you with a perfect excuse to dismount.

While one camera is usually sufficient for any bicyclist, I carried two Nikon camera bodies and three specialized lenses for the work on this book. I also brought a lightweight tripod, several red and yellow filters, a polarizing filter, and 50 rolls of film. Lense selection is important, and most people will be comfortable bringing a medium, wide-angle lense. I also took 85mm and 180mm telephoto lenses.

All three of my lenses are fast, with apertures of 1.4, 1.8, and 2.8, on the 35mm, 85mm and 180mm respectively, allowing me to photograph in low-light situations with the slower Kodachrome films which I prefer for color photography. My lightweight tripod offered me the added dimension of shooting in extreme low light, of taking a variety of blurred action shots, and of doing self-portraits.

The black and white film used in this book was Kodak Panatomic-X and Plus-X films which are enhanced if used with medium red and yellow filters. Small nylon stuff bags will help to keep all of your film and accessories together. I have often placed lenses in my spare wool socks and recommend that you have screw-on lense shades and lense filters for added protection.

Most camera equipment easily stands the test of bicycle camping. Do not hesitate to bring your best equipment. All of my Nikons continue to function perfectly, although they might appear battered and abused.

In the end, your camera will be no less a burden to you than a full water bottle or a couple of beers in your panniers. Short of reading Kerouac all over again, my experiences as a cyclist have given me the finest on-the-road adventures in my life, and my camera has wonderfully extended my fascination for the people and places to which the bicycle has led me.

*John Kelly is a photographer who lives in Basalt, Colorado, and is a partner in Russell/Kelly Photography in Aspen. He began his photographic career while serving as an infantry platoon leader in Vietnam. He has traveled extensively to photograph subjects ranging from Wimbledon Finals to African tribesmen, fashion models to Winter Olympics. Bicycling remains one of his favorite pastimes.*

*Diana Armstrong is a writer living in Moscow, Idaho. She looks forward to the time when she is connected to a bike more often than to a desk.*

# REFERENCES

## Organizations

1. **American Youth Hostels** (National Campus, Delaplane, VA 22025) AYH offers travel services and sponsors bicycle tours in the United States, Canada, and other nations. AYH membership is open to anyone, regardless of age. Members receive the *AYH Handbook* which describes the hostels, with maps, fees, and other information. There are 200 hostels in the United States, mostly in the northeast and midwest. Hostels offer inexpensive, comfortable overnight accommodations. AYH also sells mail-order bicycle and camping equipment, and books. For the catalog, write: Metropolitan New York Council AYH, 132 Spring St., New York, NY 10012. The International Youth Hostel Federation has more than 4,500 hostels in 49 member countries. Membership in AYH assures privileges in all IYHF hostels.

2. **Bikecentennial** (P.O. Box 8308, Missoula, MT 59807) "The national, nonprofit service organization for touring bicyclists," Bikecentennial hopes to have 20,000 members by 1981. Members receive the bimonthly *BikeReport*, the *Cyclists' Yellow Pages*, a discount on guidebooks, maps, and directories to Bikecentennial's developed trails, booklets on touring, and can use the Routing Service, which distributes information on bike routes in the United States. Their new Route Exchange Program enables individual cyclists to share route information. The Trans-America Trail, from Oregon to Virginia, was inaugurated in 1976. Other national trails are loops connected to the 4250-mile Trans-America. The Great Parks North and the Great Parks South link national parks in Canada and the United States from Jasper, Alberta, to southern Colorado. The Great River Route parallels the Mississippi River.

3. **League of American Wheelmen** (P.O. Box 988, Baltimore, MD 21203) "The national organization for bicyclists since 1880," LAW almost couldn't celebrate its centennial. From a high of 103,000 people in 1898, its membership dropped to 3000 in 1905 and by 1942 it was a basement, one-person outfit. Today, membership is over 10,000 and climbing. The early cycling clubs were formed for protective, as well as social, reasons. The general populace resented the relatively wealthy cyclists who could afford the expensive machines. LAW's objective is to promote cycling by supporting favorable legislation and by conducting cycling programs. Its network of local bicycling clubs supplies touring information. Members receive the monthly *American Wheelman* and the satisfaction of knowing the LAW is representing their interests in Washington. When I first heard of LAW, I figured the club was something like the Brotherhood of Elks. LAW has recently decided in favor of a long overdue name change. Not, they say, because the name was sexist, but because people might think they were motorcyclists.

4. **Canadian Cycling Association** (333 River Road, Vanier, Ontario K1L 8B9) With roots back to 1882, CCA continues to promote cycling thoroughout Canada, and conducts extensive touring programs through some regional offices. The Great Canadian Bicycle Trail, opened in 1976, runs from coast to coast. Detailed maps and guidebooks are available from CCA.

5. **Canadian Hosteling Association** (333 River Road, Vanier, Ontario, K1L 8B9) CHA has over fifty hostels and can supply various bicycle route publications.

6. **Ontario Cycling Association** (160 Vanderhoof Avenue, Toronto, Ontario M4G 4B8) Members receive the bimonthly *Ontario Cycling Scene* and route planning help. Other major Canadian provincial associations are: **Bicycling Association of British Columbia,** Suite 100, 1200 Hornby St., Vancouver, British Columbia V6Z 2E2; **Bicycle Nova Scotia,** P.O. Box 3011 South, Halifax, Nova Scotia B3J 3G6, and **Velo Quebec,** 1415 est rue Jarry, Montreal, Quebec H2E 2Z7.

7. **Bicycle Travel Bureau** (R.R. #1, Freelton, Ontario L0R 1K0) If you describe your start and destination, preferred daily mileage, type of accommodation and route, Tom Parry can provide touring information.

8. **Canadian Universities Travel Service, Dept. B.T. National** (44 St. George St., Toronto, Ontario N5S 2E4) Organizes bicycle camping tours, excellent routing, nationwide network.

9. **Bicycle Touring Group of America** (3509 Grove Avenue, Suite 3, Richmond, VA 23221) "The first collaborative effort of consumer and manufacturing interests." Its annual *Touring, U.S.A.* is available for $2.

10. **Tandem Club of America** (10 N. Lakeside Drive West, Medford, NJ 08055) Write for membership information and their newsletter.

11. **East Coast Bicycle Congress** (333 East 25th Street, Baltimore, MD 21218) The Congress provides guidebooks and maps of the East Coast Bicycle Route which goes from Virginia to Massachusetts and will eventually extend from Maine to Florida. The books contain detailed information about lodging and camping, rail connections and points of interest.

12. **Touring Exchange** (1320 Fir Villa Road, Dallas, OR) TE provides detailed information on tours that have been submitted by cyclists for other cyclists to use. Send a SASE to receive a current list of tours. Slight charge for postage and handling.

13. **Cyclists' Touring Club** (69 Meadrow, Godalming, Surrey GU7 3HS, England) CTC was formed in 1878 and is first among all touring organizations with 26,000 members. Membership earns the CTC Handbook, a tome of information about touring in Great Britain, Europe, and other countries. Their touring department will make suggestions for routes from their voluminous collection of researched tours.

# Maps

Libraries, with their national atlases, are a good place to start. They also have special map collections and unusual maps. Various cycling organizations sell guidebooks and detailed maps of specific routes. Large-scale and county maps are available from private companies. Provincial, state and county road maps are available from various departments of transportation, tourism, travel, business development, highways, and parks and recreation. These offices are in the state or provincial capitals and their addresses are available from several sources, including Bikecentennial's *Cyclists' Yellow Pages*. Some states and provinces have a coordinator of cycling activities. To find your way through cities, write the Chamber of Commerce for a city map and bicycle path guides. American Automobile Association publishes excellent general highway maps.

United States Forest Service (USFS) maps are available for each of the 154 national forests in the United States. For information on USFS maps, write to the appropriate National Forest Regional Headquarters office. If you want information about a National Park, write the appropriate National Park Service Regional office, or the National Park itself. For a list of addresses of National Parks in the United States, write National Park Service, Department of the Interior, Washington, D.C. 20240. For a list of National Forests and addresses, write National Forest Service, Department of Agriculture, Washington, D.C. 20240.

For general travel information in Canada, write the Canadian Government Office of Tourism, 235 Queen Street, Ottawa, Ontario, K1A OH6. The Canadian Government Travel Bureau, 150 Kent Street, Ottawa, Ontario K1A 0H6, will send information on camping in the national and provincial parks.

Topographical maps are accurate and detailed. Several scales are available and the best for bicycling is 1:250,000 where one inch equals four miles. Each map covers 80 to 120 miles. In the United States, write the United States Geological Survey (USGS) and request their free index for the 1:250,000 series, or write and ask for an index to the maps available for the area you plan to tour. The 1:250,000 scale maps are $2 each. East of the Mississippi write: Branch of Distribution, USGS, 1200 South Eads St., Arlington, VA 22202. West of the Mississippi, write: Branch of Distribution, USGS, Box 25286, Federal Center, Denver, CO 80225. USGS maps are available through mail-order, at USGS offices and through commercial dealers. Many libraries maintain reference files of the published maps.

For Canadian topo maps, request an index from the Map Distribution Office, Surveys and Mapping Branch, Department of Energy, Mines and Resources, Ottawa, Ontario K1A 0E9. Also, topographical maps are available from U.S./Canadian Map Service Bureau, Midwest Distribution Center, Box 249, Neehah, WI 54946. Indexes are $5.95.

Road and topo maps of Scotland, England, and other countries, are available from John Bartholomew and Sons, Ltd., 12 Duncan Street, Edinburgh EH9 1TA, Scotland. The Michelin Guides and Maps are available from P.O. Box 188, Roslyn Heights, NY 11577. The Ordnance Survey maps of Great Britain are available from Ordnance Survey, 95/D, Romsey Road, Maybush, Southampton SO9 4DH, England.

Exxon Touring Service, P.O. Box 2180, Houston, TX 77001 has road maps of Mexico and several other countries. For Latin American countries, write General Secretariat, Organization of American States, Sales and Promotion Division, 19th and Constitution Ave. N.W., Washington, D.C. 20036. Send $1 for the Pan-American Highway System map.

# Books

1. **The Ten-Speed Bicycle** by Michael Kolin and Denise de la Rosa (Emmaus, PA: Rodale Press, 1979) Lucid writing and helpful photographs and charts make this book a basic one for all enthusiastic cyclists.

2. **Richard's Bicycle Book** by Richard Ballantine (New York: Ballantine Books, 1979) Excellent repair instructions. Contains many addresses for planning a foreign tour.

3. **DeLong's Guide to Bicycles & Bicycling** by Fred DeLong (Radnor, PA: Chilton Book Company, 1978) Well-done, general introduction to bicycling.

4. **Effective Cycling** by John Forester (Custom Cycle Fitments, 782 Allen Court, Palo Alto, CA 94303, 1978) Teaching the "craft" of cycling, the section on traffic is of special interest.

5. **Clear Creek Bike Book** by Hal Aigner, Bob Jensen, Charles Powers, Lucky Wentworth, Peter Lawlor and others (New York: New American Library, 1972) Still enjoyable even though somewhat outdated.

6. **Bike Tripping** by Tom Cuthbertson (Berkeley, CA: Ten Speed Press, 1972) Section on frames by Al Eisentraut is clear and precise.

7. **The Broken Spoke** by Edward Gorey (New York: Dodd, Mead & Co., 1976) Artful drawings, macabre humor, and irreverence in the familiar, gory vein.

Touring

1. **The Bicycle Touring Book** by Tim and Glenda Wilhelm (Emmaus, PA: Rodale Press, 1980) An attractive and knowledgeable presentation of a wealth of material.

2. **The Sierra Club Guide to Outings on Wheels** by Raymond Bridge (San Francisco: Sierra Club Books, 1979) Comprehensive on all aspects of touring, a book to "look things up in."

3. **Bicycle Touring: The Complete Outfitting & Source Book** by Gail Heilman (Marshall, CA: Great Outdoors Trading Co., 1980) A buying guide with photos, lists of addresses and touring routes.

4. **Bike-Tripping Coast to Coast** by Anita Notdurft-Hopkins (Chicago: Contemporary Books, 1978) The description of the Trans-America Trail is especially valuable.

5. **Trans-America Trail Guidebooks** by Gary MacFadden (Missoula, MT: Bikecentennial) Detailed coverage of the Trans-America Trail. Five sections.

6. **Great Canadian Bicycle Trail** (Ontario, Canada: Canadian Cycling Association) Detailed coverage of the Great Canadian Bicycle Trail. Three sections.

7. **How Do You Bicycle Across Canada? Slowly, Very Slowly** by Mandy Joslin (P.O. Box 16348, Seattle, WA 98116) Bicycling the Trans-Canada Highway from British Columbia to Nova Scotia. Equipment evaluation, campgrounds, etc.

8. **Biking Alone Around the World** by J. Hart Rosdall (Hicksville, NY: Exposition Press, 1973) Account of the intrepid Australian's year and a half trip. Emphasis on Africa.

9. **Backpacking: One Step at a Time** by Harvey Manning (New York: Vintage Books, 1975) Obviously not a bicycling book, but too valuable and enjoyable not to recommend.

Maintenance

1. **Glenn's Complete Bicycling Manual** by Clarence Coles and Harold Glenn (New York: Crown Publishers, 1973) A comprehensive shop manual for the experienced mechanic. Well-illustrated.

2. **It's Easy to Fix Your Bike** by John W. McFarlane (Chicago: Follett Publishing Co., 1976) Covers basic three- and ten-speed repair. Lots of photos.

3. Manufacturer's manuals (Available from bicycle shops) These little booklets include not only assembly and maintenance instructions, but also sections on proper fitting, riding, and safety.

Food

1. **Simple Foods for the Pack** by Vikki Kinmont and Claudia Axcell (San Francisco: Sierra Club Books, 1976) Wholesome recipes for home, trail or road.

2. **Cooking on the Road** by John Rakowski (Mountain View, CA: World Publications, 1980) Rakowski's extensive experience as a hungry cycle tourist has helped create a book as satisfying as the recipes prove to be. Very useful.

3. **Joy of Cooking** by Irma Rombauer and Marion R. Becker (New York: Bobbs-Merrill, 1975) The best all-around general cookbook.

Massage

1. **Do-It-Yourself Shiatsu** by Wataru Ohashi (New York: E.P. Dutton, 1976) Superb illustrations.

2. **The Massage Book** by George Downing (New York: Random House, 1972) A classic.

3. **The Foot Book: Healing the Body Through Reflexology** (San Francisco: Barnes and Noble, 1977) Well-written.

# Periodicals

1. **Bicycling** (Rodale Press, Emmaus, PA 18049) Nine issues a year. Features product review, road tests, articles on diet and health, long and short tours, comment and opinion. An annual subject index is available.

2. **BikeReport** (Bikecentennial Box 8308, Missoula, MT 59807) Bimonthly to members. Tabloid format. Concerns cycle touring in the United States.

3. **American Wheelmen** (League of American Wheelmen, P.O. Box 988, Baltimore MD 21203) Monthly to members. Contains club news, schedules of events, medical advice, reports on legislation of interest to cyclists.

4. **Ontario Cycling Scene** (Ontario Cycling Association, 559 Jarvis Street, Toronto, Ontario M4Y 2J1) Bimonthly to members. Tabloid format. Touring emphasis. Booklets on aspects of touring available. Send SASE and money for postage.

5. **Cycle Touring** (Cyclists' Touring Club, 69 Meadrow, Godalming, Surrey GU7 3HS, England.) Six times a year to members. European cycling companions may be requested through the publication by writing to the editor, H. John Way.

6. **Cyclists' Yellow Pages** (Bikecentennial, P.O. Box 8305, Missoula, MT 59807) Resource guide to maps, books, routes and organizations. Annotated. One dollar for non-members.

7. **Bicycle Resource Guide** (David J. Leubbers, 78 S. Jackson, Denver, CO 80209) Lists current (1979) English language bike literature. Absolutely encyclopedic, it has everything from books through governmental documents to publications of foreign tourist organizations and films. Addresses and brief annotations. $5.

8. **The Touring Cyclists' Hospitality Directory** (John Mosley, 13623 Sylvan, Van Nuys, CA 91401) Compilation of persons who have offered simple hospitality to touring cyclists. U.S. and Canadian listings. To receive the directory, you must be listed. Send a SASE and a contribution for postage and handling.

9. **LAW's Hospitality Homes** (League of American Wheelmen, P.O. Box 988, Baltimore, MD 21203) If you would like to offer accommodations to tourists who pass through your area, write LAW. The list appears annually in LAW's membership directory.